Notice to Subscribers

Immigrants, Refugees, and U.S. Policy is number 6 in Volume
52 of The Reference Shelf. It has been substituted for the previously announced title on the subject of money, which has been
delayed to a later volume.

IMMIGRANTS, REFUGEES, AND U.S. POLICY

edited by GRANT S. McCLELLAN
Editor, CURRENT Magazine

THE REFERENCE SHELF

Volume 52 Number 6

WYOMING VALLEY WEST HIGH SCHOOL

THE H. W. WILSON COMPANY

New York   1981

THE REFERENCE SHELF

The books in this series contain reprints of articles, excerpts from books, and addresses on current issues and social trends in the United States and other countries. There are six separately bound numbers in each volume, all of which are generally published in the same calendar year. One number is a collection of recent speeches; each of the others is devoted to a single subject and gives background information and discussion from various points of view, concluding with a comprehensive bibliography. Books in the series may be purchased individually or on subscription.

Library of Congress Cataloging in Publication Data

Main entry under title:

Immigrants, refugees, and U.S. policy.
    (The Reference shelf; v. 52, no. 6)
    Bibliography: p.
  1. United States—Emigration and immigration—
Addresses, essays, lectures. 2. Refugees—United States
—Addresses, essays, lectures. I. McClellan, Grant S.
II. Series: Reference shelf ; v. 52, no. 6.
JV6455.I55   325.73   81-749
ISBN 0-8242-0653-3   AACR2

Copyright © 1981 by The H. W. Wilson Company. All rights reserved. No part of this work may be reproduced or copied in any form or by any means, including but not restricted to graphic, electronic, and mechanical—for example, photocopying, recording, taping, or information and retrieval systems—without the express written permission of the publisher, except that a reviewer may quote and a magazine or newspaper may print brief passages as part of a review written specifically for inclusion in that magazine or newspaper.

PRINTED IN THE UNITED STATES OF AMERICA

CONTENTS

3

PREFACE

Mass movements of people—refugees or other migrants—across national borders have in recent years intensified. The impact of those movements, global in range, is of special concern to the United States, with its history as a haven and land of promise. The worldwide scope of the current migrations is attested to by the flow of over a million refugees from Indochina and Afghanistan and from Cuba and Haiti in only one year. The issues raised are not new, but fresh attention has been focused on the latest arrivals at the Federal level and also in the regions most affected, notably California and the other Southwestern states and Florida.

The purpose of this compilation is threefold: to outline the general problems resulting from the huge influx; to raise specific issues relating to the immigrant groups—their impact on the economy, the mistreatment of some, the barriers of diverse languages and cultures; and to present formulas that might provide humanitarian solutions yet ease the burdens placed upon the American people.

Section I is concerned with the general immigration picture today. Section II deals with various migrant groups and enclaves: Hispanics, Chicanos, Miami as a Latinized city, Cubans in New Jersey, Cape Verdeans in Massachusetts, Haitians, Asians in New York City, Soviet Jews in Brooklyn, the Los Angeles melting pot. Section III focuses chiefly on the thorny cultural and educational question of bilingualism. Section IV looks ahead, suggesting possible future policies.

The editor wishes to thank the authors and publishers of the selections that follow for permission to reprint them in this compilation.

Grant S. McClellan

December 1980

NOTE TO THE READER

For other views on immigrant ethnic groups, the reader is referred to Marjorie P. K. Weiser's *Ethnic America* (Reference Shelf, Volume 50, Number 2), published in 1978.

I. AMERICAN REACTIONS TO A WORLD PROBLEM

EDITOR'S INTRODUCTION

The articles in this section provide a general view of our immigration and refugee problem today—how Americans perceive the problem and how official policy reflects those perceptions.

The first selection, by Warren M. Christopher, Deputy Secretary of State in the Carter Administration, looks at the resettlement of displaced people as a global issue with special significance for the Western Hemisphere. Next, Margot Hornblower, of the *Washington Post*, surveys the United States as an "irresistible magnet," its force still powerful despite rising opposition to aliens today. The development of government refugee policy is covered by Connie Wright, in an article from the *Nation's Cities Weekly*.

That undocumented workers are exploited as a cheap labor force is the contention of Roger Waldinger, of the MIT-Harvard urban studies center, writing in the *Democratic Left*. What to do about the vast number of illegal aliens is taken up by an article from *Black Enterprise*. A related question—whether aliens crowd the job field—is the subject of another New York *Times* article, by Peter Applebome.

In the last article, William L. Chaze, an associate editor of *U.S. News & World Report*, discusses today's conflicts and tensions, with refugees stung by a backlash of native resentment and clamor for restrictions and reform.

REFUGEES: A GLOBAL ISSUE[1]

Earlier this month [July 1980], the Secretary General [of the Organization of American states] referred to the OAS as

[1] Reprint of statement by Deputy Secretary Warren M. Christopher before the Permanent Council of the Organization of American States (OAS), Washington, DC,

a forum for dialogue on important world and hemispheric issues. I appreciate this opportunity to join that dialogue on an issue of growing concern to us all.

I refer to the global issue of refugees—to the problems that follow the abrupt, massive, induced displacement of persons. Such migrations may result from wars, natural disasters, persecution, or other local conditions. Whatever the causes, they raise deep legal and humanitarian issues. And these issues are fitting concerns for the international community and this Organization.

Our governments will shortly begin intensive consultations on this problem. Today, therefore, I will outline the challenges we face as a backdrop for actions that this forum, or others, may consider in the future.

The problem of refugees and displaced persons is serious, widespread, and—I regret to say—growing. More than 15 million inhabitants of our planet have fled their homes in recent years because of wars, civil disturbances, persecution, or hostile government policies. They include more than 7 million Asians, 4 million Africans, 3 million from the Middle East, and 300,000 Europeans. Perhaps most pointedly for the people in this room, they include 1.2 million people of our hemisphere.

In a few cases, fortunately, these odysseys have proved temporary. The settlement of the Zimbabwe conflict enabled nearly 200,000 men, women, and children to return to their homes. In our own hemisphere, a similar number of Nicaraguans, who had fled to neighboring countries, returned home once the civil war ended in that country.

Sadly, however, such happy endings are relatively rare. The past year alone has witnessed the flight of more than 1.2 million Afghans, 1 million Somalis, and hundreds of thousands of Kampucheans and others who remain homeless and miserable. Ours is becoming an epoch of refugees.

Today, as a consequence, few countries can be confident

July 23, 1980. (Current Policy no 201) United States. Department of State. Bureau of Public Affairs. Office of Public Communication. Washington, DC 20520. '80. p 1–4.

that they will not suddenly face refugee problems originating outside their borders. And no one country, however well-intentioned, can deal by itself with large-scale flights of refugees. As this problem transcends national boundaries, so should the solution transcend single nations.

Since 1975, the United States has welcomed over 600,000 refugees for permanent resettlement. In the past 10 months alone, we have taken in 230,000 refugees; and this total does not include the 150,000 Cubans and Haitians now in the United States, seeking to settle here. We are doing everything we can to assist refugees from around the world who look to us for help. But we need help if we are to help them.

Cuban Refugees

A new and critical dimension of this problem developed for the United States in April of this year. At that time, the first of what are now more than 115,000 Cubans began arriving on our shores. The salient facts are these:

☐ In April, more than 10,000 Cubans seeking asylum crowded into the Peruvian Embassy in Havana. An airlift was organized by Costa Rica and several international agencies; but Cuba abruptly ended the airlift before it could be completed.

☐ As a consequence, many of the refugees from the Peruvian Embassy, and thousands more, were induced to depart in small and dangerously overloaded boats. Few of those boats meet even minimum safety standards. The ensuing boatlift brought great suffering; a number of lives were lost at sea.

☐ The Cuban refugees who did reach our shores included many who do not qualify for admission under our immigration laws. At least 1,000 among them are known to have committed serious criminal acts. Many of them were released from jail on the specific condition that they would leave for the United States.

☐ Cuba has rejected repeated efforts to work out safe, orderly, legal procedures so that Cubans may emigrate to countries willing to receive them. These include bilateral representations by the United States and other nations; multilateral contacts through responsible international agencies; and the effort of a tripartite group formed at the international conference in San Jose last May. All have been rebuffed.

☐ Last month, the United States formally sought to repatriate 65 Cubans who had asked to return to their country. That effort, too, was rebuffed.

☐ In May, several hundred Cubans seeking to come to the United States in full conformity with our immigration laws were set upon and beaten in front of the U.S. Interests Section in Havana. More than 300 of them sought temporary sanctuary inside; and to this day, most of them remain in our Interests Section.

☐ Finally, as you are aware, the chaotic flow of Cubans into the United States has dropped off sharply in recent weeks. This has been primarily due to vigorous preventive efforts by my government. Yet the fundamental problems remain: thousands of people eager to leave that country; the refusal of Cuba to cooperate in devising orderly, legal arrangements for dealing with this migration; and the massive burdens that are imposed when thousands of people migrate under such adverse conditions.

Role of the Inter-American Community

I should like to suggest that in this deeply affecting situation, the entire inter-American community has an important role to play. One challenge is to resettle those Cubans who have come to the United States but who do not have strong ties with this country. For example, at least 800 Cubans now in refugee centers here have made clear their interest in settling in other countries. We will continue to look to the hemisphere to play a role in their resettlement.

Another challenge—and one of even greater long-term significance—is to develop and reinforce legal instruments which more adequately spell out the rights and obligations of states in dealing with refugee problems.

There are some grounds for optimism. The generous hospitality of Honduras, Costa Rica, and other Central American countries during the recent Nicaraguan civil war enabled almost 200,000 people to find refuge. Assistance from international and regional organizations and neighboring countries helped the Central American nations deal with this crisis until the end of hostilities enabled the refugees to return to Nicaragua.

Similarly, many nations in the hemisphere have made generous contributions toward resolving the problems posed by the exodus from Cuba. Argentina, Peru, Ecuador, Costa Rica, and Venezuela, among others, have received or offered to receive Cuban migrants. Costa Rica made a generous offer to receive Cubans for onward resettlement. Costa Rica also played a leading role in establishing the unfortunately short-lived "air bridge" and called two international meetings to discuss means of regularizing the Cuban exodus.

The two San Jose conferences constitute an unprecedented international effort to give effect to certain basic precepts of international law—precepts designed to protect the rights of individuals as well as the rights of states. It is, for example, a fundamental principle of customary international law—incorporated in many international conventions—that persons may not be transported in disregard of the immigration laws of the receiving state. No government has the right to select emigrants for permanent resettlement in another country. This right to establish and enforce national immigration laws is grounded in the principles of mutual respect and equality of states which are the foundation of all international law. Needless to say, the international export of convicted criminals is a particularly egregious violation of this elementary principle.

Moreover, each nation has a corresponding duty to receive its own citizens who have been expelled by another state. This obligation is clearly spelled out in modern treaties for the protection of human rights.

Nations must also, of course, observe the basic safety requirements set forth in the International Convention for the Safety of Life at Sea. But as we have already noted in the

Maritime Safety Committee of the Inter-governmental Maritime Consultative Organization, the vessels which formed the Mariel sealift were deliberately overloaded; they did not meet convention safety standards. The U.S. Coast Guard, in fact, rescued a large number of those who left Cuba via Mariel.

Need for a Worldwide Response

The challenges I have outlined—and others arising from refugee migrations—require a concerted response in this hemisphere and in the world community. In the past, the Organization has set precedents that other regional bodies and the United Nations have later adopted. Today, the inter-American system is again well-situated to make a similar contribution.

In the past few years, movements of people fleeing their homelands have touched all our countries. Such mass movements of people are likely to continue with potentially serious repercussions for each of our societies. To date, however, we have developed no mechanism to cope with massive waves of displaced people or with countries which induce such displacements in violation of basic international norms.

A global and humanitarian problem of such sweep requires our best collective efforts. On behalf of my government, I would suggest four principles that might well guide our collective search for a solution.

First. Large-scale displacements of persons should be discouraged in the name of humanity and international order. I can imagine no justification—political, social, racial, or religious—for a government to induce large numbers of its citizens to flee their homeland.

Second. Persons displaced from their homelands should be repatriated, as promptly as conditions permit. Permanent resettlement should not be accepted as the inevitable result of crisis, for such permanent displacement may serve neither the welfare of the individuals or the nations concerned. The repatriation of persons following the end of the fighting in Zimbabwe and Nicaragua demonstrates that there are effective and humane alternatives to permanent resettlement.

Third. International procedures must be devised to solve the problems which arise when permanent resettlement becomes necessary. In such situations, the task of resettlement should be shared on an equitable basis so that no single nation or group of nations is faced with the entire refugee burden. Any system for resettlement must take into account that displaced persons are truly an international problem requiring an international solution.

Fourth. Our efforts must be focused on the fundamental human issues involved. These issues are too serious to be made the subject of partisan or ideological polemics.

Developing Cooperative Machinery

In developing the elements of such an international solution, we might well begin by reaffirming the principle of mutual respect for immigration laws. A concrete way of doing this would be to develop cooperative machinery to prevent the misuse of vessels and aircraft in refugee migrations. We should also reaffirm the absolute obligation of states to permit the return of their citizens.

We should, in addition, consider ways in which the inter-American system can help international relief organizations, private voluntary organizations, and other agencies in their efforts to deal with future crises.

The OAS can work closely with international agencies like the U.N. High Commissioner for Refugees and the Intergovernmental Committee for European Migration to develop procedures for coping with these complex and highly sensitive problems. The OAS might, for example, provide the institutional framework for insuring that appropriate legal obligations are carried out and that member nations get the help they need to meet their responsibilities to displaced people. Our efforts to develop regional procedures to control dangerous and chaotic refugee flows could set a precedent for larger international efforts to deal with this global problem.

Conclusion

In conclusion, I would like to suggest that we of the Americas can take the lead in responding to this grave humanitarian problem. And I should like to suggest that in the weeks ahead, we focus our efforts in two directions.

First. Toward the immediate problem: What role can the OAS play to assist the permanent resettlement of persons now in countries of first asylum? We should specifically consult on whether an OAS Permanent Council meeting should address this problem.

Second. Toward the long-term issue: What norms and mechanisms can be established to deal with future problems of this nature? Our consultations should focus in particular on how to involve the OAS General Assembly in efforts this fall to develop such norms and mechanisms.

The United States looks forward to the day when all peoples can live happily, peacefully, and productively in their own countries—a day which unfortunately is not yet in sight. Meanwhile the community of nations, of which the OAS is a vital institution, must develop remedies that will protect the rights of people and of nations and serve the cause to which all of us are dedicated—the cause of peace, stability, and cooperation among the nations of the world.

A MAGNET FOR MILLIONS[2]

Arabs have immigrated to Detroit, Salvadorans to Washington, Haitians to Miami, Kurds to Nashville. America on this Fourth of July is more than ever a nation of nations.

At least a million immigrants and refugees will pour into the United States this year—perhaps as many as any year in America's history. About 700,000 will come legally—Soviet Jews, Vietnamese boat people, Cuban political prisoners.

[2] Reprint of article by Margot Hornblower, staff writer. Washington *Post*. p. A1+. Jl. 4. '80. Copyright © 1980, The Washington Post. Reprinted by permission.

Hundreds of thousands more—no one knows for sure how many—will sneak over the Mexican border or fly into Dulles Airport as "tourists," and melt into the economy as illegal aliens.

Irish potato famine, Hungarian revolution, Indochinese war—the United States, whatever its ambivalence toward the role, has long served as the safety valve for international crises, welcoming more immigrants and refugees than all other free-world nations combined.

American prestige may be dwindling in the eyes of global leaders, but for the oppressed or poverty-stricken people of the world, this country remains an irresistible magnet. Four million a year get in line to come to the United States. Waiting lists for certain types of visas are backed up 11 years.

A Kettering Foundation study in the early 1970s reported that one-third of the people in Latin America want to emigrate here. Indochinese refugees in Thailand overwhelmingly choose the United States over other countries.

The unexpected flood of 117,000 Cuban boat people this spring, coupled with the continuing influx of Indochinese at the rate of 14,000 a month, focuses sudden public attention on immigration.

With the freedom flotilla coming ashore in Key West, Fla., the Carter administration woke up to discover it didn't really have an immigration policy. As Victor Palmieri, the State Department's refugee coordinator, put it, "We can't afford to take them all in. We can't keep them out."

America has historically welcomed "the huddled masses yearning to breathe free." It is part of the national identity.

"The bosom of America is open to receive not only the opulent and respectable strange," George Washington said in 1783, "but the oppressed and persecuted of all nations and all religions."

Nonetheless, from the 19th Century "yellow peril" scare, prompting laws excluding Asians, to recent efforts of immigration officials to deport Haitians, each new immigrant wave has brought political backlash.

Today, with unemployment nearing 8 percent, the

thought of spending millions of dollars to resettle outsiders
has riled many Americans. In California and Texas, lawsuits
have been filed to stop the states from granting medical and
other social services to illegal aliens.

The reaction is ironic, because every American—Indians
excepted—is descended from an immigrant, and many quite
recently. The 1970 census found that 34.5 million Americans
were either foreign-born or had one or more foreign-born
parents.

While some unions complain that illegal aliens and new
immigrants steal jobs from American workers, studies show
that many of the jobs they take are low-paying ones that
Americans don't want—domestics, dishwashers, lettuce
pickers. Entrepreneurial Cubans are credited with reviving
Miami's economy in the 1960s—creating more jobs for everyone. Soviet Jews have rejuvenated Brooklyn neighborhoods
that were turning into slums.

Some economists see an increase in immigration as a
boon. Because of the recent slide in the American birth rate,
the number of workers in the U.S. labor force is expected to
decline, beginning in 1982, as fewer young workers come of
age.

One thing has changed dramatically since the years when
Ellis Island served as the gateway to America for millions of
refugees traveling steerage across the oceans. Unlike their
predecessors, the new immigrants are increasingly from Third
World countries, challenging American society to broader
racial and cultural tolerance.

Changing Attitudes

Meanwhile, attitudes have changed in the past two decades. The idea of the melting pot, in which all nationalities
would blend into a homogeneous stew, is no longer fashion-
able. Ethnic has become chic.

American women dress in Mexican skirts and Indian
shawls, cook with woks and send their children to bilingual

schools. Ethiopian, Afghan and Vietnamese restaurants are the rage in Washington and other big cities. Arab bread is sold in the Safeway. The most popular Bicentennial event in small midwestern towns four years ago was the ethnic festival.

Immigrants are more inclined than ever to cling to their heritage. Spanish-speaking Mexicans, Puerto Ricans and Cubans have created cities within cities in such places as Miami and San Antonio. Theirs is a culture that doesn't wash away with the passage of generations, a culture that demands equality with Anglo America.

In Los Angeles, where 50 percent of kindergarten children claim Spanish as a first language, all police cadets are required to take six months of conversational Spanish. Miami blacks complain they can't get jobs because they don't speak Spanish.

But every ethnic group experiences the pangs of culture clash, the pull of its American future and the tug of its past, whether the group be composed of Russian Jews, Hmong tribesmen or Cape Verdeans from West Africa.

And for each group the experience is vastly different. The Cubans, who grew up playing baseball and selling cigars to wealthy Americans, have an easier time adapting than the Hmong, who lived isolated from the world in the mountain villages of Laos.

Virtually every group reports family tensions exacerbated by the quicker adaptability of the young and the nostalgia of the old. Vietnamese parents complain that their children talk back to them, a habit learned from American friends. Cuban parents complain of the sexual freedom of American youth. Young Cape Verdeans, whose parents think of themselves as Portuguese, now call themselves Afro-Americans.

In the eyes of Conrad Tauber, a census expert, becoming American can mean going full circle. "The first generation tries to maintain its culture," he has said. "The second generation—kids born of foreign parents—reject it as much as they can. The third generation is still somewhat resentful of

ethnicity, but the fourth generation is proud of it. They can
stage a Norwegian festival and dress up in folk costumes and
go back to being good Americans the next day."

THE DEVELOPMENT OF REFUGEE POLICY[3]

Over the years, the American way of accepting newcomers from abroad, helping them get resettled and giving
them aid and comfort has become a perplexing task for the
nation and its communities.

Though the country was settled and expanded with an
open-door policy, by 1875 national leaders decided there
should be restrictions: the first immigration law barred such
persons as prostitutes and convicts.

In 1921, we became even more particular: country-of-
origin quotas were enacted, and visas were assigned according to yearly immigration limits. Reflecting our population
patterns of the time, the system made it relatively easy for
applicants from northern and western European nations,
harder for those in southern or eastern Europe and almost
impossible for Asians.

There was no official distinction for "refugees," apart
from other immigrants, until after World War 2. In 1945,
with camps full of people displaced by the war, private voluntary agencies here began to push for their admission to the
United States.

These groups helped bring about the Truman Directive,
which admitted displaced persons under existing quotas by
giving visa preference to refugees over non-refugees. The voluntary agencies agreed to meet the costs of resettlement. Refugees entered the country as "parolees," a conditional status
that later could be adjusted to "immigrant" status.

[3] Reprint of article entitled "The Refugees: How Policy Developed over the
Years," by Connie Wright, staff writer. *Nation's Cities Weekly.* 3:1+. Ag. 11, '80.
© 1980, The National League of Cities. Reprinted by permission.

The first large-scale application of this parolee status covered about a third of the 40,000 Hungarians who arrived after the abortive anticommunist rebellion in 1956. The rest were admitted under regular quotas.

A White House committee coordinated resettlement for the Hungarians, but there were no complex federal support systems. They had a well-established community already settled here, and they were able to find jobs easily in a time of low unemployment. Most settled in New York, New Jersey, Pennsylvania and Ohio.

In 1959, Fidel Castro's success in Cuba brought on this country's longest-lived refugee resettlement program. In earlier programs, refugees had been processed for travel from camps in other countries, allowing sponsoring agencies and communities to prepare for their arrival. The Cubans came directly to the United States.

Partly because of distaste for World War 2 refugee camps, the United States did not restrict movement, residence or employment possibilities for these Cubans. Many stayed in Florida, but others moved and formed neighborhood self-help groups in cities throughout the country.

Today, Cuban-American communities are helping the recent Cuban arrivals. In Houston, "the new wave of Cubans are doing well," reports John Castillo, assistant to the mayor, "because the older group is helping them."

Across the country, however, the scene was not always so smooth. With 10,000 or more Cuban "parolees" arriving each year, there was a substantial drain on already hard-pressed public agencies and private groups. Federal aid programs were available only to those meeting strict eligibility and residency requirements, and payments were low. Nothing was available for those who were unemployed or who were unable to work.

In Miami, city officials formed a Cuban Refugee Committee to appeal for federal assistance, suggesting to President Eisenhower that refugees should be considered a national responsibility. Shortly afterward, contingency funds to assist

the Cubans were authorized from the International Cooperation Administration, forerunner of the Agency for International Development.

In 1961, federal involvement in refugee resettlement became much more substantial. Refugees were entitled to the
same benefits as citizens; assistance was channelled from the
Department of Health, Education and Welfare to states and
voluntary agencies.

The quota system was dropped in 1965, but a new law still
limited total immigration from non-Western Hemisphere
areas to 170,000 persons yearly. Applicants in certain categories would be allowed to come first, including those who had
special skills, relatives here or a need for political asylum.

The attorney general still could allow "parolees" to enter
the country. This provision was intended for isolated, emergency cases, not for handling large groups.

Cuban refugees continued to be admitted as parolees.
Most overstayed their period of admission and were permitted to remain indefinitely; by the mid-1970s they numbered
750,000, according to a report by the New TransCentury
Foundation in 1979. By that estimate it is the largest long-
term refugee movement in U.S. history.

In 1975, the collapse of the Saigon government brought a
sudden mass migration, challenging American communities
to meet their needs. Almost overnight, 130,000 refugees were
evacuated to Guam and then to resettlement camps here, according to an estimate by the Indochina Refugee Action Center in Washington. The Office of Refugee Resettlement in the
federal Department of Health and Human Services says there
are 380,000 Indochinese refugees here now.

Reaction among Americans was mixed—partly because of
the recent long military involvement in South Vietnam. Hostility was more pronounced than it had been for earlier refugee groups. Conflict and confusion occurred as various organizations and communities sought to help the Vietnamese.

Congressional reaction also was mixed. Concern was expressed about health and employment issues—and the fiscal
impact of so many refugees on the nation's communities. As a

result, Congress designed the Indochina Refugee Assistance Program to provide cash, medical assistance and social services to Indochinese refugees through federal agreements with state and local public and private agencies. School systems provided language training with the funds.

The refugee resettlement program was originally considered an emergency measure; funding was appropriated on a year-by-year basis. It was a decentralized system that involved many federal, state and local governments. Many who participated in it said in the last few years that new refugee legislation was overdue.

The Refugee Act of 1980

The Refugee Act of 1980, signed into law in March, was the first major reworking of American immigration law since 1965. It made significant changes in refugee admission and resettlement policies, mostly by providing uniform funding and coordination of refugee programs and services.

Among the law's major provisions:

"Refugee" is redefined as any person forced to leave his or her home in any part of the world because of race, religion, nationality, political opinion or membership in a particular social group. Previously, the term was applied only to those who came from communist countries or the Middle East.

The number of refugees allowed into the country each year has been raised to 50,000 through fiscal year 1982; the president may increase this quota, after consulting with Congress. (The figure doesn't include about 14,000 Indochinese refugees per month, who are being admitted to fulfill a commitment the administration made in July 1979 to a United Nations conference in Geneva.) About 228,000 refugees are expected to enter the country in fiscal year 1980.

An immediate benefit of the law is predictable financing. Voluntary agencies, in the past, have not always known how much federal assistance to count on. It also has eased admission of unaccompanied refugee children. Previously, there had been a gap of legal responsibility for them between their departure from camps and their acceptance as wards of the state in which they finally settled.

Just a month after the new law was enacted, it was put to the test. More than 3,000 Cuban refugees suddenly arrived by boatloads on Florida's shores; they were treated as parolees and given 60 days to apply for political asylum. Asylum procedures involve a case-by-case review, a process that can take months. The Refugee Act did not authorize federal assistance to those awaiting final action on their asylum claims, except for those who applied by November 1, 1979. "Clearly, these provisions were not written with the kind of situation in mind that we face today," Ambassador Victor H. Palmieri, the U.S. refugee affairs coordinator, told the House Judiciary Committee April 30. The statement was incorporated among the official policies reprinted in his "Refugee Resettlement Resource Book," currently in draft form.

"With this current influx of undocumented arrivals fleeing from Cuba, we are experiencing the pressures of being a country of first asylum—a burden that we have borne before in our history," Palmieri said. "Like scores of first-asylum countries around the world today, we will be generous. We will be sensitive to the basic human desires that motivated their flight: No boats will be turned away, and no one will be returned to a country where he or she would face persecution," he promised.

Newspapers across the nation featured scenes of havoc in Florida's Dade County communities, where the Cubans were housed in temporary shelters. Since they were not considered refugees under the new definition, the task of resettling them became much more difficult for the cities and counties where they were to eventually settle. City officials began to wonder how they would cope when they already were strained with fiscal problems. Many of the new Cubans were single men needing jobs—men with no relatives or sponsors to support them.

The public and its officials wonder how the refugees can be accommodated in their communities in an orderly way, when the evening television news shows them rioting in a federal camp in Pennsylvania over rumored mistreatment of a pregnant woman, and when American cities already are scarred by disturbances said to be fueled by officials' inadequate attention to needs of residents who are not recent refugees.

The Haitian Newcomers

Another group of newcomers, the Haitians, have been trickling steadily into Florida since 1972. Immigration and Naturalization Service officials say there are about 20,000 Haitians in the Miami area; an equal number, they say, are uncounted. Records show they have been treated differently, as few have been given permanent resident status, and charges of racism have come from civil rights groups.

The administration justifies the different treatment by asserting that the Haitians are simply fleeing poverty. Most Haitians arriving here are black, unskilled and often illiterate. The Cubans have been predominantly middle class.

Some help came in late June, when the administration announced a new policy on assistance to the more than 129,000 recently arrived Cubans and Haitians, establishing a Cuban-Haitian "entrant" status. Under this classification, the newcomers are eligible for federally financed programs. State and local governments must pick up part of the costs.

A supplemental appropriations bill, signed July 8, contains $100 million appropriated to the president for special migration and refugee assistance in fiscal years 1980 and 1981. Without resolving the legal status of Cubans and Haitians, the law will partially reimburse federal agencies and state and local governments. It also grants more funds to other refugee resettlement programs.

In addition, the White House has proposed legislation that would provide 75 percent reimbursement for medical assistance, special educational programs, social services and other general aid for one year.

"While new laws facilitate the entry of refugees and provide access to needed services, they cannot guarantee acceptance once the newcomers arrive in local communities," says Ron Scheinman of the Select Commission on Immigration and Refugee Policy, a national panel established by the president and Congress.

"We can talk about concepts like 'acculturation' and 'assimilation' and provide money and programs to set refugees on their feet," he adds. "But what refugees need most of all is acceptance and a feeling of being welcomed. That goal can only be achieved through coordination, open communication and good will at the local level."

THE PLIGHT OF UNDOCUMENTED WORKERS[4]

The influx of Cuban refugees [in the spring of 1980] exemplified the complexities and misunderstandings that bedevil immigration policy. While makeshift rescue operations were mounted off the Florida shore, the Carter administration vacillated, unsure of the proper reaction to this latest wave.

After considerable indecision, Carter bowed to the inevitable, ceasing to restrict the flow and assisting in the process of resettlement. The aftermath of this episode has provided little occasion for self-congratulation. Resettlement has been agonizingly slow. Exploitation of refugees at the workplace has already been reported. And most importantly, the eruption of the Liberty City ghetto in Miami sparked in part by resentment at the reception accorded the refugees, suggested to some policymakers and analysts that the tolerance level for immigrants is relatively low.

The pessimistic and conventional view is that the U.S. is being flooded by the world's poor and oppressed. Although this is merely a refrain from the bad old restrictionist past, the anti-immigrationist argument has been updated. The modern-day kicker has it that America's homegrown poor are the

[4] Reprint of article entitled "Undocumented Workers: Exploited and Resented," by Roger Waldinger, a Fellow at the Joint Center for Urban Studies, MIT-Harvard. *Democratic Left.* 8:16–19. S. '80. Reprinted by permission.

ones most likely to be hurt. And to close the circle, it is argued that economic competition between immigrants and low-income natives will kindle social conflict of a type—to quote the usually sober *Business Week*—"that will make the riots in Miami look like a Boy Scout campfire."

Reality, however, departs quite sharply from these myths. Today's immigrants are not so poor, and their numbers, relative to total U.S. population, not as great as popular opinion would suggest. Their arrival, moreover, is not so closely linked to the deterioration of conditions in the home countries as it is to the demand for low-wage labor bred by the U.S. economy. Doomsayers to the contrary, the employment of immigrants at the bottom of the labor market is unlikely to throw many Americans out of work, let alone endanger the "social fabric."

Who Are the New Immigrants?

Today's immigrants, as distinguished from refugees, are conventionally treated as two different groups: the legal immigrants, and the undocumented. The first are those who arrive with legal resident status. This is granted to immigrants who have close family ties (as children, spouses, and siblings) to American citizens or legal alien residents, and to a lesser extent, to immigrants with particularly valuable skills and talents not available in the United States. The undocumented are immigrants who either evade inspection when crossing into the country at the borders or enter the country with a visa and then remain beyond the limits of their stay. Most of the Mexican undocumented immigrants belong to the first category while most of the other Western Hemisphere and Eastern Hemisphere undocumenteds are, in immigration parlance, "overstays." The distinctions between the two groups are not great. Indeed, many legal immigrants are former "illegals," a fact that suggests that the dynamics of the two migration currents may be similar.

The major change in the legal immigration flow dates to the 1960s. Prior to 1965, legal immigrants were primarily western and northern Europeans. With the abolition of the national origins system in 1965, Third World immigrants came to predominate. In 1977, the last date for which we have statistics, the legal stream was 34 percent Asian and 44 percent Latin American and Caribbean. Only 15 percent of the 1977 legal immigrants came from Europe.

Compared to the legal immigrants who came at the turn of the century, today's immigrants are more heavily white collar (more than 30 percent of the legal immigrants with previous work experience held professional or managerial jobs prior to immigration), far less likely to be of rural origins, and predominantly female (53 percent of the 1977 immigrants were women). Moreover, the relative size of today's immigrant flow is dwarfed by that of the past. An average of 1,100,000 people arrived on these shores between 1903 and 1913, an influx that accounted for over 40 percent of the growth of the labor force during that period. During the 1970s, legal immigration ranged from a low of 370,000 in 1971 to last year's high in the 700,000 range, with no distinct trend appearing until refugee movements in the late seventies caused a pronounced upwards tilt. Prior to the refugee influx, approximately 230,000 legal immigrants entered the labor force annually. Even with the refugee addition taken into account, the total number of new immigrant workers remains overshadowed by the size of the active workforce of almost 97 million.

Unfortunately, any statement about undocumented immigrants must be made with little degree of precision. The accepted estimate puts the undocumented population in the four to six million range. It had been thought previously that the overwhelming majority were from Mexico. However, a recent Census report argues that at least half of the undocumented immigrants are non-Mexican, primarily from the Caribbean and Latin American countries.

Of course, not knowing how many immigrants are here and where most of them are from greatly complicates the task of describing them. We know most about the Mexican immigrants, though even here the picture is not clear. These immigrants are primarily, though not entirely, from rural areas: although ex-farmworkers are disproportionately represented, the immigrants come from the broad middle to rural Mexican society. The poorest, for the most part, are not part of the migration stream. Unlike the legal migrants, these undocumented workers are predominantly male; the female proportion, however, is apparently increasing.

Why They Come

We tend to look at the phenomenon of immigration through a very personalized prism. With the exception of Native Americans and most blacks, we are the descendants of "voluntary" immigrants. What follows from this inheritance is a particular set of assumptions: that America has acted as a land of refuge for those impelled to leave their countries of origin; and that the act of immigration is one and the same with the process of settlement. These assumptions, however, are contradicted by the historical record and their implications for contemporary developments are equally misleading.

Migration during the last great wave at the turn of the century does not conform to currently held notions. Apart from the Jew—who did fit the idealized image of a group fleeing intolerable political and economic conditions—there was little migration of family units. Obscured today by the haze of time, it was the "bird of passage" phenomenon that impressed contemporaries. Like the swallows after whom they were named, a significant portion of the turn-of-the-century immigrants passed annually back and forth across the Atlantic in response to seasonal fluctuations in their trades. Thirty to forty percent of those who left Italy, the Baltic, and the Balkans returned to their homes after a sojourn in the U.S. And for many who did establish permanent residence, the decision to do so was clearly a consequence of, not a prelude to, their encounter with the new land.

A similar pattern holds true today. Much of the Mexican undocumented immigration is temporary in nature. Emigration from Mexico to the U.S., as University of California political scientist Wayne Cornelius has argued, can be linked to conjunctural swings in the rural economy that lead peasants and farm workers to seek a reprieve through labor in the U.S. As was the case for the migrants "imported" by the advanced European countries during the 1960s and early 1970s, many Mexican undocumented workers migrate to earn money to buy land, agricultural implements, a truck, or some other consumer durable upon return home. To some extent, the term "immigration" in the accepted sense is a misnomer when applied to the Mexican case. In some Mexican villages, even the acquisition of legal immigrant status does not lead to a shift of residence. Rather, it serves as a pass for "professional migrants" to enter the U.S. for temporary stays and then return home for the greater portion of the year.

The prevalence and continuity of temporary migration suggests that immigration is primarily rooted in conditions in the U.S. itself, and only secondarily in the emigrating countries. As Michael Piore, an economist at MIT, has argued, industrial societies have a tendency to create jobs that can only be filled by searching for new sources of labor supply, a quest that historically has led to the importation of migrant workers. At the turn of the century, rapid economic growth and the burgeoning of relatively unskilled jobs in manufacturing industries led to massive immigration.

After World War I curtailed European immigration, U.S. employers sought new workers for bottom-level jobs. This search precipitated the black exodus from the South and provided the catalyst for the Mexican migration northwards that has continued to this day.

The current wave is a recapitulation of earlier migrations, induced and influenced by similar factors. The uneven development of the U.S. economy perpetuates a large number of low-wage jobs in traditional manufacturing industries while multiplying the number of dead-end, undesirable jobs in the service sector. Huge inequalities of pay—in 1976, for example, eleven million jobs paid at or near the minimum wage— make many jobs undesirable for native workers with other sources of income support (public assistance, training programs, etc.). It is in precisely this range that the immigrants are placed. One of the most comprehensive studies available, a survey of over 800 apprehended undocumented workers, found that the undocumenteds were relegated to bottom-level jobs in the low-wage sector and that their earnings fell below those of U.S. workers employed in comparable jobs. Other sources confirm this picture.

On the supply side, there is both continuity and change. In the industrial heartland and in the Northeast, the traditional sources that have fed into the bottom of the low-wage labor market have changed. In the 1960s, black and Puerto Rican migration northward tapered off; in the 1970s, these currents halted or reversed. As this process has been played out, employers have sought labor elsewhere: particularly in and around the Caribbean basin.

In the Southwest the story reads slightly differently. There, where undocumented workers have traditionally been employed in agriculture, economic expansion has widened demand. One research team studying five towns in northern Mexico found that agriculture provided employment for 84 percent of those migrants who worked in the U.S. prior to 1969, but only 45 percent of those who have sojourned here since then.

Since the new immigration began it has obtained a dynamic of its own. The pull from the U.S. has been powerfully reinforced by the contradictions of development in neighboring countries. Relying heavily on capital intensive plans that have accelerated growth without producing commensurate gains in employment, many of the countries in the U.S.-bound immigration stream have displaced traditional jobs without creating domestic alternatives. Severe under- and unemployment have thus combined with disparities in the distribution of income to enlarge the current headed towards the U.S.

The immigration current has been strengthened further as well-established networks channel information and job-finding assistance to new migrants and the existence of immigrant communities eases the tasks of finding shelter and employment. Finally, the back and forth flow of temporary and permanent immigrants, as well as the sending of remittances, have spread the U.S. model of consumption throughout the sending countries, making U.S.-bound migration a part of the culture.

Market Impact

The controversy over the impact of immigration has focused narrowly on the question of cost. Observers and partisans ask whether the new immigrants, particularly the undocumented, displace American workers and thereby aggravate the level of economic distress.

The preceding analysis strongly suggests that the answer to this question is no. This view first emphasizes the origins of the new immigration and the conjunctural developments that precipitated it. In this instance, the declining unemployment rates, gains in employment, alternative job opportunities in manpower training programs, and improved public assistance benefits loosened the constraints that bound workers to the low-wage sector. These developments reverberated in the workplace, leading workers to resist customary conditions and practices and inducing employers to look for a more tractable labor force.

The second, related, argument has to do with the nature of work in the low-wage sector. Employment at the bottom of the occupational ladder is compatible with the needs and aspirations of temporary migrants, who are most interested in accumulating savings in order to return home. The same holds true for the first generation, which judges current status and earnings in relation to conditions they lived under prior to migration and not to the norm in the U.S. These comparative factors, however, exercise little sway over the second generation, who opt out of the traditional immigrant jobs of sewing, dishwashing, cleaning, and the like. The critical point is that the faltering of the post-war migration waves, as discussed above, and the maturation of the second generation, cleared the way for the entry of a new low-wage labor force.

If concern over employers substituting undocumented

workers for otherwise employed natives is misplaced, fear that undocumented migration might coincide with a decline of basic working conditions seems well-founded. Once again the usual caveat—about the inadequacies of the data base and conflicting reports—must be injected. But the evidence is compelling enough to indicate that certain segments of the low-wage sector are poised for a return to the sweatshop.

The most comprehensive picture comes from an intensive investigation of low-wage industries conducted by a special branch of the California Department of Labor. Of 3,253 workplaces inspected, 59 percent were found to be in violation of basic labor standards. In the garment industry, a major employer of immigrants that has largely managed to keep the International Ladies' Garment Workers' Union at bay (only 10 percent of the California garment workforce is organized), payment of sub-minimum wages, homework, and child-labor were particularly flagrant.

A similar impact has been felt on the East Coast. The Employment Standards Administration, which has intensified its efforts to police the labor codes in a series of low-wage industries, has uncovered abuses in construction, services, light manufacturing, and especially garments.

How should this reversion to substandard conditions be interpreted? To some extent, there has been erosion of labor standards throughout American industry, a trend which bears no direct relationship to immigration: 1979 set a record for labor standards violations. Immigrants are heavily employed in industries where competitive pressures are severe; in some, such as garments, the intensification of international competition has heightened the labor cost constraints.

More important, perhaps, has been the shifting character of government regulation. Historically, the labor standards mandate was focused on the low-wage sector. In the past twenty years, however, the jurisdiction of government agencies in this field has been widened without commensurate increase in staffing or funding. More critical yet, the policing of the labor codes has suffered from a dual barrage: the right's assault on government regulation in general, and the crunch of the fiscal crisis. The imprint of the former can be seen in the enforcement of health and safety codes. The Occupational Safety and Health Administration acts within a narrow cost-benefit calculus that leads it to focus on high hazard industries or serious violations where there may be imminent danger. In practice this means that there is virtually no surveillance of the "low-risk" industries where the immigrants congregate. Clearly, the passage of such restrictive legislation as the Schweiker amendment will cripple enforcement in industries where the threat to workers' health is grave, but not the most severe.

The fiscal crisis has been an equally great hindrance. In New York State, for example, the squeeze on state expenditures has cut personnel in the Division of Labor Standards by almost one-half and severely restricted the agency's capacity to do more than respond to complaints. Other public departments with authority over building and fire conditions, for example, have been equally enfeebled.

As pressures on labor costs are intensifying and state control is diminishing, the number of undocumented workers in the low-wage sector has increased. Bereft of the rights and protections enjoyed by citizens and legal alien residents, the undocumenteds are easy prey to employers who have little to fear and much to gain from exploitation.

Labor's Response

Since the early seventies, anti-immigrant ardor has cooled off, particularly within the liberal-left, which has had conflicts on this issue. The most important factor in this process has been the presence at countless workplaces of the undocumenteds themselves. As they have encountered immigrants, a number of unions—the now-merged Amalgamated Meat Cutters, the Steelworkers, the Garment Workers, and the Electrical Workers, among others—have attempted to organize them, albeit with limited success. Often, Immigration and Naturalization Service (INS) agents have squashed promising organizing campaigns by stepping in just before a representation election or during the course of a strike. The ILGWU, whose membership is heavily immigrant and which must organize large numbers of undocumenteds on both East and West Coasts, attempted to directly counter the influence of the INS by filing (an ultimately unsuccessful) suit to halt factory raids and by pressuring union employers to bar admittance to Immigration agents.

Within the past two years, this experience in the field has percolated into policy. Labor has become more vocal in its defense of the alien and more sympathetic to a liberal readjustment of status for the undocumenteds. At a news conference following the February 1980 AFL-CIO Executive Council meeting, Lane Kirkland endorsed a "broad and sweeping amnesty for those (undocumented immigrants) who are presently in this country."

Discerning the prospects for this or any other policy change is particularly difficult. For much of the last decade, the political initiative rested with Congress. The Carter administration, however, was at first determined to take some action and developed a legislative package in its first year of office. Its proposals included an amnesty for undocumented immigrants residing in the U.S. prior to 1970, a penalty for employers hiring undocumented workers, and a guestworker program similar to those operated in Europe prior to 1973. As with other Carter proposals, this one was issued with fanfare, only to die silently in Congress. Since then, little action has been forthcoming.

What then, are the implications of the new immigration and the policy debate for labor and the left? The agenda should clearly be shaped by some simple demographic facts. Immigration is changing the complexion of the workforce and population in vital sectors and regions. In California, there are 450,000 legal alien residents of Mexican origin. During the first half of the 1970s, the legal alien resident population of New York City increased by 30 percent. With considerable growth registered since then, recent immigrants not yet naturalized now comprise a significant proportion of the city's population.

In addition to the legal aliens there is a population—of indeterminate size—of undocumented immigrants that seek permanent residency. This is a potentially major constituency. Equally important, it is a group with particular needs and aspirations that are currently neglected and undefended.

Continued political immobility and the deterioration of conditions at the bottom of the labor market make defense of the alien a priority. An interim strategy should focus around strengthened enforcement of labor standards and rejuvenated organizing.

The long-term options are far more problematic, primarily because the policy goals are so unclear. The current debate assumes that a restrictionist solution is the desired outcome. But if the analysis developed here is correct, none of the commonly proposed restrictionist mechanisms is likely to slow the current immigration tide so long as the underlying inequities in the occupational structure persist. However, by implying that greater equality will eliminate the utility of a workforce willing to accept jobs that natives decline, this same argument makes the left a friend of the immigrants, but not a supporter of a greatly opened door.

THE INVISIBLE INVASION[5]

Since 1820, more than 48 million immigrants have come to America in search of the good life. The Irish came to escape the potato famine of the 1840s. Jews from Eastern Europe and Russia saw this country as a refuge from poverty and anti-Semitism. The underclasses of Italy and other European nations were participants in one of the greatest migrations of all time—14.5 million in the first two decades of this century.

They all came during a time when the Statue of Liberty was the symbol of an unprecedented generosity: a beacon for

[5] Reprint of article from *Black Enterprise.* 10:29–30. Ap. '80. Copyright 1980, The Earl G. Graves Publishing Co., Inc. 295 Madison Avenue, New York, NY 10017. All rights reserved. Reprinted by permission.

the "tired," the "poor," "the huddled masses yearning to breathe free." But as our country has aged and our economy grown more uncertain, we have become more selective in our choice of immigrants.

The United States admits 400,000 legal immigrants each year under fixed quotas and several hundred thousand others who are refugees or under special categories. However, there are thousands who cannot get in legally but who still see America as the land of opportunity. The result is a vast and invisible army of undocumented immigrants, or "illegal aliens," who have settled all over the country and live with the constant fear of expulsion.

The magnitude of the problem is best illustrated by the inability of US officials to determine just how many illegals are here. "We could count them if we could catch them," says Vern Jarvis, a spokesman for the US Immigration and Naturalization Service (INS). Estimates run as high as 12 million. The latest study by the Bureau of the Census suggests the actual number to be closer to 6 million and possibly as low as 3.5 million. Last year, more than a million illegal aliens were apprehended, but the same individuals are often arrested over and over again. Most illegals come from Mexico, South America, and Asia, but large numbers also come from Haiti and the Dominican Republic.

The concern of Americans about these uninvited guests is tied to economic cycles. When business is good, undocumented aliens get little attention but when the economy falters, public concern focuses on the illegals. In the West and Southwest, middle-class whites—and blacks— blame Mexicans for everything from rising crime rates to strained social services. In the Midwest and East, Caribbean and Latin American immigrants are accused of taking jobs away from Americans. "I can't get work because the West Indians are freezing everyone out of the field," complains Daryl Kelly, a 23-year-old mechanic's helper from Brooklyn, NY. "Most of the black Americans won't work for less than $7 an hour and the West Indians will take half that amount."

Late in January, INS investigators ordered passengers off
several suburban buses leaving New York's Port Authority
Bus Terminal and seized 85 Caribbean-born illegal aliens.
Most of them were working as domestics in New Jersey
homes. Many labor unions—even those with undocumented
aliens on their rolls—argue that the willingness of undocumented aliens to accept low wages undermines their bargain-
ing power because they are a source of cheap, unorganized
labor. "Those workers who won't join a union because they
fear detection and deportation are being forced into a new
underclass," says Jay Mazur, president of Local 2325 of the
International Ladies' Garment Workers' Union. "The only
way to deal with this problem is to grant them total amnesty."

But not all labor officials are as sympathetic toward the
undocumented. William Pollard, a high-ranking black official
of the AFL–CIO, has argued for tougher laws on the grounds
that poor blacks are being hurt by the flood of undocumented
aliens. Pollard's sentiment is supported by those who feel that
illegal aliens benefit from social services and schools already
strained by declining tax rolls and inflation.

But experts like Wayne A. Cornelius of the Mexican Studies Center at the University of California in San Diego argue
there is little real evidence that immigrants and non-immi-
grants are in direct competition for low-paying jobs. "We

ALIENS ADMITTED LEGALLY	
North America (includes Mexico and the Caribbean)	187,345
Asia	157,759
Europe	40,010
South America	32,954
Africa	10,155
Oceania	4,092
Source: U.S. Immigration and Naturalization Service (1977)	

have found that immigrants often put more into the system than they get from it," says Cornelius. "For obvious reasons, many of them do not take advantage of tax-funded programs although they are taxpayers."

"The immigrant is not the enemy," says Cornelius. "It is unfortunate that certain segments of the black community have bought this argument." But Cornelius also reports that most illegal aliens have entered service industries "where the bulk of low-scale jobs in our economy are."

Sandy Close, editor of Pacific News Service in San Francisco and a frequent writer on immigration issues, points out that the percentage of black males permanently out of work jumped from 20 to 30 percent in the last decade—the same period that saw a big jump in legal and illegal immigration.

"The real competition for blacks has come out of legal immigration," she says, "in the areas which require certain skills. Most illegal aliens have moved into the secondary (lower-wage) labor market where the ability to move around is a major asset. The real question is how you organize the secondary labor market so there is real job stability and job security and guarantee that blacks get their fair share."

Nearly everyone agrees that it is virtually impossible to stop the flow of illegal aliens because of our thousands of miles of unguarded borders. But an important first step toward formulating a fair immigration policy is to determine just how many illegal aliens are in the country.

Cities that have been losing population want the US Cen-

ALIENS EXPELLED FROM U.S.	
Mexico	998,830
El Salvador	11,414
Canada	7,426
Guatemala	4,421
Colombia	3,574
Source: U.S. Immigration and Naturalization Service (1979)	

sus Bureau to count the illegals so they can avoid losing federal funds and seats in Congress. The Bureau has made extensive plans and enlisted the help of minority leaders in an effort to make an accurate count. But five members of Congress have joined private citizens in a suit demanding that the 1980 Census distinguish between legal and illegal aliens. If the Bureau goes ahead with plans to count the illegals, they argue, California, New York, Texas and three other states with large populations of illegal aliens would gain congressional districts at the expense of 13 other states.

To fulfill a campaign promise to Mexican-Americans, President Carter submitted a controversial immigration reform plan to Congress in 1977 that called for amnesty for the 765,000 illegal aliens estimated to be in the country before January 1, 1970 and temporary five-year work permits for an estimated 5 million illegal aliens who had been in the country before January 1, 1977. Mexican-American leaders denounced the plan as inadequate and it never reached the floor of either house of Congress.

Some experts believe that the only real solution is to strengthen the economies of neighboring countries. Most illegal aliens come from Third World countries (see chart) with weak economies and high unemployment rates. The discovery of large oil reserves in Mexico could eventually reverse years of exodus by Mexican peasants seeking the better life. But the problems of Caribbean and Latin American countries with few valuable natural resources are more severe and there are no short-term solutions.

The doors to America were wide open until the 1920s when a failing economy, the fear of foreign-born radicals and the resurgence of racism prompted Congress to limit immigration. Quotas favored northern Europeans over Mediterranean peoples and whites over non-whites. The laws were reformed in the 1950s and have been amended since. But they have left inequities such as those faced by Haitians, who cannot be admitted because they come from a "friendly" country, while thousands of Cambodians, Russian Jews and

Cubans are welcomed because they are escaping from communist countries.

There is little doubt that America cannot absorb all those who would like to come here, but our concern about the economic impact of illegal aliens can obscure the human dimensions of the issue. "Many undocumented aliens look at a job here as their last chance to climb out of poverty and a hopeless life, and a last chance to bring their families out of it," says George Montoya, chief of general investigations for the INS in New York. "You can feel like you're taking hope away from a man when you find him."

The question before Americans is one that we have grappled with for half a century. Which tired, which wretched, which poor should be given a chance to become good Americans?

DO ALIENS CROWD THE JOB FIELD?[6]

When 29-year old Dock Green lost his job on the management-training squad at a fried-chicken franchise [in Dallas], the first telephone call he made was to the United States Immigration and Naturalization Service.

"I realized I was in trouble right from the start when I saw that I was the only one there who spoke English. Everyone else spoke only Spanish," Mr. Green said. "I kept complaining to my boss that all these people were illegal aliens, and he didn't want to do anything about it.

"I have nothing against those people, but every day we had people coming in asking about jobs, and it's a pitiful shame to have people who are born and raised here be out of work, and have these illegal aliens taking their job. To me, the

[6] Excerpts from article entitled "Do Aliens Fill a Need or Crowd Job Field?" by Peter Applebome, a regular contributor to the New York *Times* from Dallas. New York *Times*. Section 12 (National Recruitment Survey), p 45+. O. 12, '80. © 1980 by The New York Times Company. Reprinted by permission.

law means what it says, and if those people are illegal, then the law should be obeyed."

Mr. Green is not alone in his frustration. Illegal aliens are playing an increasingly visible role in the job market, a role subjected to rising criticism at a time of relatively high unemployment of Americans.

But Hispanic leaders and many academics insist the impact of those workers is essentially benign. They say Mexican workers who cross the 1,300-mile border into the United States do the menial jobs Americans don't want, are essential for the harvesting of crops, and use very few municipal services while filling the lowest niches in the job market.

Ruben Bonilla, president of the 100,000-member League of United Latin-American Citizens, said undocumented workers, in addition to playing a positive role in the economy, actually increase tax revenues by paying for Social Security service they seldom use. He said any crackdown on Mexican immigration would have a much more harmful effect than any displacement of Americans from available jobs that goes on now.

"If we close the border, I feel that Mexico would literally burst at the seams," he said. "When you look at Mexico's 30 percent inflation and crippling unemployment, it's clear these people have nowhere else to go. If they couldn't leave, I think social conditions in Mexico could become so bad there would be the loss of the democratic republic in Mexico as we know it. I don't think America would want a Socialist or Communistic nation any closer than Cuba."

Most experts would agree with Mr. Bonilla that Mexicans and other aliens fill manual tasks that are the least desirable in the job market. But many of those same experts also would agree with Mr. Green that there is no shortage of Americans competing for many of those jobs.

Proposals to deal with the flood of illegal aliens in the job market have ranged from tighter border patrols, to sanctions against employers who hire illegal aliens, to temporary work visas that would allow a limited number of aliens to work here legally. Even those calling for one policy or another concede there is no way to be sure how many illegal aliens are in the work force or what their effects have been.

"I don't have any hard data and I don't know anyone who does," said Dr. Vernon Briggs, a labor economist at Cornell University, who has studied illegal immigration since the mid-1960s. "But it can't be in the best interests of this country to have a whole population of people who are without rights, people who can't vote, people who have to live in constant fear of detection. It's becoming a problem we can't ignore any longer even if we wanted to."

Estimates on the number of illegal aliens vary from 6 million to 12 million, but despite the lack of hard figures, some trends are clear. The vast majority live and work in three states, California, Texas and Florida, and two cities, New York and Chicago. Most of them come here for one reason: to work.

Most illegal aliens work in agriculture, restaurants, or hotels. Mexico, which sends an estimated 500,000 illegal aliens into this country every year, is the biggest source. Other aliens come from Cuba, Haiti, the Dominican Republic, Hong Kong, the Philippines and dozens of other nations, but experts estimate 60 percent of illegal aliens in the country are Mexican.

Dr. Briggs, who became interested in illegal aliens after trying to help organize farm workers in south Texas in the 1960s, said his research shows illegal aliens compete with Americans for jobs in all industries in which they are represented, at the same time depressing wages and blunting moves toward unionization or improvement of working conditions.

"The studies that have been done show the employment patterns of illegal aliens in the Southwest are very similar to those of other Chicanos in terms of geography and occupation. We've built this whole phantom labor source into the labor market and someone must show what they do if not compete with the available labor force."

A Neo-Slavery Institution

One matter that is not in question is the conditions under which illegal aliens live. Francisco Barba, a San Francisco lawyer who has defended hundreds of illegal aliens, told the Select Commission on Immigration and Refugee Policy, a group created almost two years ago to study immigration policies, that "immigration labor today is America's neo-slavery institution." Federal investigators in recent years have documented hundreds of cases of abuse of illegal aliens. A Federal Department of Labor strike force investigating treatment of illegal aliens in Houston, Dallas and Forth Worth this year uncovered $1.2 million in underpayments owed 4,470 employees, most of them illegal Mexican aliens. Officials said the investigation involved only a tiny percentage of illegal aliens in the area. . . .

Supporters . . . [of legislation allowing the Government to fine employers who knowingly hire illegal aliens] say sanctions are the most effective way to keep aliens out of the labor market. Some opponents say sanctions would make employers do the job of the Immigration and Naturalization Service. Others say aliens are essential in some industries—primarily farm work—where there is not an adequate supply of Americans who will do the work. And Hispanic leaders say sanctions would prompt employers to discriminate against all Hispanics.

REFUGEES: STUNG BY A BACKLASH[7]
Reprinted from *U.S. News & World Report.*

Since World War II, more than 1.4 million refugees from all over the world have fled to U.S. shores, the vast majority of

[7] Reprint of article by William L. Chaze, associate editor. *U.S. News & World Report.* 89:60-3. O. 13, '80.

them moving into the mainstream of American life and finding the opportunities they sought.

In the past two years, however, an influx of 465,000 newcomers, mostly from Indo-China, Cuba and Haiti, has brought problems that have led to growing hostility.

Far from finding the promised land of their dreams, large numbers of the latest refugees have encountered a backlash that is taking many forms—from Miami whites angrily protesting the resettlement of more Latins in their midst to Californians complaining about having to compete with Indo-Chinese refugees for factory jobs.

Today, a growing number of Americans are saying the U.S. has welcomed more than its share of political refugees, as well as ordinary immigrants, and should pull up the gangplank. Housing and jobs, they say, are in short supply and must be reserved for Americans.

In a nation of immigrants, some arrivals are finding an increasingly cold reception. "I expected little when I came from Laos—only the right to earn a living and support my children," said Trang Duc Ky of San Francisco as he fished for his evening meal off a pier near Golden Gate Bridge. "Most people show me kindness, but I sometimes see hate in the eyes of people as I walk the streets. It saddens me."

Flickering on and off since the Vietnamese began arriving in 1975, animosity in the U.S. ripened into anger over the summer with the arrival of 123,000 more Cubans aboard the "Freedom Flotilla." Fidel Castro finally slammed shut Cuba's doors in late September, but Haitians continue to pour into Florida at the rate of several hundred a week. At the same time, the influx of Indo-Chinese is on the increase, the result of President Carter's doubling their quota to 168,000 annually.

Even so, anti-refugee feeling does not run uniformly deep throughout the country. It is concentrated mostly in large cities, where the bulk of refugees have settled. In many smaller communities, refugees have been warmly welcomed and praised for their industry and spirit—but even in those places a single incident often turns congeniality into hostility.

Historic Bias

Hard feelings toward immigrants are nothing new in the U.S. On the contrary, the nation has displayed a strong, grassroots bias against refugees for much of its history. The official policy has always been one of welcome—it is emblazoned on the Statue of Liberty—but history books are full of stories about how Irish, Chinese and Eastern European immigrants were mistreated in the 19th century.

"There is a gangplank mentality here, and we are seeing evidence of it now," says Msgr. Bryan Walsh of Miami, long active in refugee affairs. "Once a group of immigrants arrives and settles in, they tend to want to crank up the gangplank and keep others out. We're even seeing it among Cubans."

Surveys present clear evidence of the backlash. A recent Roper Poll, for instance, showed 80 percent of Americans favoring cutbacks in immigration quotas—a figure that will reach 217,000 in 1981, not counting "forced refugees" like the Haitians and Cubans. That is fewer than the U.S. was taking in a century ago, but still twice as many as the rest of the free world admits on a combined basis.

The anger is being fed by worry over how the U.S. will cope with the flood of refugees. All told, more than 375,000 Indo-Chinese, 900,000 Cubans and 100,000 Haitians are now in the United States. On top of that—while they are not classed as refugees—there are millions of illegal aliens, most of them from Mexico and South America. Estimates range from 3.5 to 12 million.

Refugee costs are staggering. In 1981, taxpayers will shell out over a billion dollars in aid, apart from local-government costs not returned by Uncle Sam. Orange County, Calif., for instance, with 75,000 Indo-Chinese, computes its costs at 3 million dollars a year. For Miami and surrounding Dade County, Fla., the bill is 4.2 million dollars for health care and social services.

At Miami's Jackson Memorial Hospital, a Haitian baby is born every 6 hours, generally at taxpayer expense—a matter of some local resentment. "Our backs are to the wall," says

Dade County official Eileen Maloney. "People are burned up about it."

Anti-refugee sentiment is running so high in South Florida that citizens have managed to get on the November ballot a proposal to end Dade County's official status as bilingual in Spanish and English. "It is mostly symbolic, but still a highly emotional issue," said David Leahy, the county's deputy supervisor of elections.

In September, the President moved to defuse the problem in Florida, ordering a processing center opened in Puerto Rico for Cubans and Haitians. Two thirds of all Cubans, plus most of the Haitians who have come to the U.S. in recent months, stayed in Florida—a deluge of 150,000 in less than a year. Earlier, Carter ordered sent to the Fort Chaffee, Ark., resettlement camp the 10,000 refugees being processed at three other camps across the country. The other centers will be closed in October.

A troubled U.S. economy is helping sour some citizens on the refugees. Many Americans are concerned about being displaced by foreigners who, they fear, will work more cheaply than themselves. Not only are lower-income Americans competing with refugees for jobs but also for that rarity in the U.S. today—cheap housing.

On top of all this, there has been a steady stream of bad publicity about the new arrivals, both Latin and Asian. The stories have left the strong impression that the newest refugees are a bad element. "Right now, all refugees are being tarred with the same brush," says a regional official of the U.S. Department of Health and Human Services in California. "These days, a refugee is a refugee, and it makes no difference whether he is from Cuba or Laos. He's looked upon as bad news. Most are good people, but they have a bad image."

Scars from Cubans

The Cuban resettlement program has blackened the eyes of all refugees, regardless of origin. Even the most generous critics of the effort describe it as a shambles, a far cry from the programs stitched together to help others in times past. "There's a feeling in Congress, just like among the people in Florida, that the whole thing has run amok," asserts Senator Lawton Chiles (D-Fla.).

Some observers say that the changing nature of Cuban refugees is at the root of the problem. Where earlier ones were mainly professional people and businessmen, the latest exiles are largely poorly educated blue-collar workers from small towns and rural areas. At least 5,000 have admitted to prison records, and many are avowed homosexuals. Says Richard Erstad, a Quaker relief worker in Philadelphia: "The trouble is that some have no family connections, few skills and probably were misfits in Cuba."

Relief agencies have found it hard to line up sponsors for the refugees, leaving many to languish for six months in re-settlement camps in Florida, Wisconsin, Arkansas and Pennsylvania. At all four places, outbreaks of violence, sparked by boredom and cramped conditions, have caused bad feelings on the part of nearby residents.

"In this part of Pennsylvania, a Cuban is mud," said a relief worker at Fort Indiantown Gap, Pa. "They are seen as troublemakers. You couldn't find a sponsor for one in these parts if you had a million dollars. There was dancing in the street when local people heard the camp would be closed."

Further aggravating the situation: The hijacking of seven commercial airliners by disgruntled refugees who wanted to go back to Cuba and the September arrest of a Cuban man in Tomah, Wis., on charges of slaying his sponsor, a 56-year-old woman. "We're trying to keep things cool here now," said a Tomah policeman. "A lot of local people are upset. We're worried about them taking out their frustrations on Cubans who stray from the camp. We're going to have to protect them, though they had nothing to do with this."

Roving Gangs

The Indo-Chinese have generated fewer headlines, but they have also reaped a share of unfavorable publicity. Police in Los Angeles and neighboring Orange County say young Vietnamese men, unable to find work, have organized roving gangs that specialize in street crimes. Most victims have been other Asians.

In San Francisco, residents were outraged in August by reports of Laotians and Cambodians stalking squirrels, ducks and stray dogs in Golden Gate Park and eating their catch. "They are hunting this park and trapping the wildlife," says Joe Bestresky, assistant park superintendent. "They eat anything that moves. People don't understand that it is part of their culture."

In Fairfield, Iowa, last January, a Laotian man tried to kill himself, his wife and three children. A son died. Since then, no more Indo-Chinese families have been invited to settle there. "It turned people off," says Larry Johnson, managing editor of the local newspaper. "There's been talk about Cubans—but no offers of sponsorship."

Most Indo-Chinese coming to the U.S. are uneducated farmers who, in addition to speaking no English, are unschooled in city ways. Many are illiterate even in their own language. Not only must they cope with the shock of a new homeland, but also with an urban life that can be confusing for natives. "They try to follow the old ways, and people often don't understand," comments San Francisco journalist Dexter Waugh. "If people don't understand, they get hostile. It's like the park poaching. Back when it was middle-class hippie kids doing it, nobody gave a damn."

With few exceptions, the newest Asian and Latin refugees have settled in crowded urban areas where housing is a major problem. It also is a point of friction between immigrant groups competing for the same limited space.

In Denver, for instance, Latins reacted violently when 24 Indo-Chinese families were given apartments in a Chicano housing project with a long waiting list of Hispanics. After incidents of rock and bottle throwing, other housing was found for the Asians. The Chicano complaint: Latins waited months for space given to the Asians. State officials have since made it clear they want no Cuban refugees.

The same tensions are building elsewhere, too. "I came to San Francisco to find work, but before I get work, I need a place to live," says Steven D. Early, a black construction worker from Little Rock, Ark. "Only place I can afford to live is skid row. But now you can't get in there because of the Vietnamese. Can't find a cheap place any more because refugees have them all. Makes a man mad as hell."

For the Vietnamese, the problem is made even more acute by the outright refusal of some landlords to rent to them. "I go to many, many places before I find a white man who will rent me an apartment in a neighborhood that is not Laotian," said Wang Duong Tri of Los Angeles. "People take one look at me and take down the vacancy sign. They say big mistake, no room." In Seattle, Wash., a local property owner tells of a caller who asked if he rented to Vietnamese. Informed that he did, the caller exclaimed: "Thank God. We've looked everywhere, and you are the only one who would rent to us." The story is the same for Cubans and Haitians. In Miami and Union City, N.J., many sleep on park benches and in alleys.

Job Competition

The search for work is another source of conflict with their new countrymen. In Santa Clara County, Calif., known as "Silicon Valley" because of its concentration of electronics plants, thousands of Indo-Chinese have found work. But with the economy worsening, some local people are beginning to fret about whether they will be crowded out by newcomers.

"It could get tough if the economy keeps on winding down and jobs get harder to come by," says Paul E. Smith, an assembler in a transistor plant. "It doesn't seem fair to me that native Americans should have to compete with Cubans and Vietnamese for work. I wish them well, but not at my expense."

Tensions still run high between Vietnamese and American fishermen off the Texas coast. The Americans deeply resent having to compete with refugees for fish, and the feelings have occasionally exploded into violence. In 1979, one American was shot to death. Other clashes have left serious injuries on both sides. "It is still a volatile situation," said a state refugee official. "It will remain that way so long as we have too many fishermen and too few fish."

Richard Livingston, a Volunteers in Service to America worker in San Francisco, believes most Americans would be more sympathetic to the plight of refugees if only they understood the difficulties the newcomers must surmount. "They often endure terrible hardships—extreme poverty, loneliness. It can be hellish."

Typical is the situation of Ung Kong-Mon's family, which lives in a seedy apartment house in San Francisco's tough Tenderloin area. Their neighbors on Leavenworth Street are prostitutes, derelicts and drug pushers. Winos in filthy tatters stagger down the dimly lighted hallway at high noon, and shouts and curses from adjoining apartments often awaken the family at night. The playground for children is a rat-infested hallway, littered with debris. For most people, it would be a bleak setting of utter despair—but for Kong-Mon, his wife and four children it is a place of hope.

The family has been in San Francisco for 10 months, living on $722-a-month welfare. Kong-Mon has been going to language school and looking for work, walking miles each day to and from Chinatown. Soon, he hopes to land a job. "We look around and it is not what we want—many bad people and hard times," says his wife. "But our eye is on the future. We know that this will pass. We will become important people in time, good citizens. We are willing to work hard."

Aiming for Success

Examples abound of refugees who have achieved the good life in the United States. When Lap Huynh and his family arrived here from Vietnam in 1975, they had no more than a few pieces of clothing. Today they are the owners of one of the San Francisco area's finest French restaurants.

Three years after his arrival from Vietnam as a penniless

refugee, Tung Duong is a successful insurance man who recently bought his own home. In Miami, Cubans own more than 18,000 businesses. More than 3,500 are physicians, 16 are bank presidents, 250 are bank vice presidents. Carlos J. Arboleya, whose first job in the U.S. 20 years ago was in a shoe factory, is now president of the Barnett Bank of Miami. "It can be done," he says. "But it is not easy."

A federal study recently showed that, on average, immigrants start earning more than native-born American families within 10 years of arriving in the United States. Conducted for the Select Commission on Immigration and Refugee Policy, the study indicates that it usually takes less than six years for an immigrant family to earn as much as a native family. At the same time, the survey shows that immigrant families pay into the Treasury more in taxes than they take out in welfare and other services.

Nonetheless, the commission will recommend early in 1981 a sweeping overhaul of the nation's immigration laws. One likely recommendation: An annual cap of 500,000 to 1 million on all newcomers. Any surge of special refugees would have to be balanced by an equal cut in the numbers of other immigrants. Under emergency provisions of the present law, the President may admit an unlimited number of refugees.

Immigration reforms are likely to find wide favor on Capitol Hill—so long as they are tough ones. Pressure is already building for stricter limits, and lawmakers report they get more mail from voters on refugee problems than on any other national issue. Says Senator Richard Stone (D-Fla.): "It's hard to overstate the social upheaval and backlash that have developed over this problem. We're more and more aware of this in Congress."

But solving the human problem of refugees like Guillermo Diaz, 28, a former Havana trash collector, is likely to take longer than for the legislative mill to crank out a new law. Along with 700 other Cubans, he spent a month living in a dusty and noisy tent city beneath Miami's expressways.

With a prison record for petty theft, Diaz has no prospects of a regular job. He owns only the old clothes on his back, and sleeps on park benches, doing odd jobs for small amounts of money. "America," he says in broken English, "is not what I hoped for. I do not know if I will do so well here. I think it will be a fight for survival."

Copyright 1980 U.S. News & World Report, Inc.

II. VARIED GROUPS AND SPECIAL NEEDS

EDITOR'S INTRODUCTION

As illustrated in the general discussions of the preceding section, the magnitude of the national immigration problem is aggravated by its demographics—the diversity of the tide of newcomers and the localized impact of their arrivals. The articles that follow detail the severe pressures experienced by diverse groups and by the regions that have felt the greatest effects of today's influx.

First, Geoffrey Godsell, of *The Christian Science Monitor*, depicts Hispanics in the United States as an ethnic "Sleeping Giant." Next, Griffin Smith, Jr., in a *National Geographic* excerpt, reports on Mexican Americans—their heritage and their changing place in American society.

The Latinization of Miami is analyzed by Herbert Burkholz in an excerpt from the New York *Times Magazine*. Accounts of two local groups follow: a report on Cubans in New Jersey, by Washington *Post* writer Donnel Nunes, and on Cape Verdean migrants in Massachusetts, by Kathy Sawyer, also of the Washington *Post*.

A selection from *The Christian Century* by Paul Lehmann outlines the plight of Haitian "boat people" seeking asylum in Florida. New York City provides a refuge for two other groups—Asians, whose life is described by Anna Quindlen of the New York *Times*, and Soviet Jews, whose Brooklyn enclave is covered by Dusko Doder of the Washington *Post*. The section concludes with Laurel Leff's *Wall Street Journal* observations on Los Angeles, as the new melting-pot metropolis of a nation of immigrants.

HISPANICS IN THE UNITED STATES[1]

The Hispanic giant in the United States is awakening and coming out of his labyrinth of solitude—to use the evocative phrase coined by Mexican poet Octavio Paz.

As he stirs himself, this giant will continue to get bigger.

What is happening was unwittingly summed up by a diminutive elderly Mexican-American woman from one of the barrios (Hispanic neighborhoods) that sprawl for miles eastward across the Los Angeles River from downtown Los Angeles. (East Los Angeles is the home of more people of Mexican origin than are to be found in any other urban concentration except for Mexico City itself.) The woman had just come from a meeting last year of 1,200 members of the area's United Neighborhoods Organization with Los Angeles Mayor Tom Bradley. Well-briefed and awesomely organized, this remarkable delegation from the barrios had gone to the meeting determined to get from the mayor his signed agreement to cooperate with them in securing much-needed funds for better housing. They got it.

A few years ago, this elderly woman would never have dreamed of doing anything but passively accepting the often-hard lot of those living in the barrios. But after the triumphant meeting with Mayor Bradley, she said: "Before, I used to think of Mayor Bradley as tall and powerful. Today I feel as tall and powerful as he."

This is a feeling only just beginning in the Hispanic communities across the US. For the full national political and social consequences of it, and for the development of an effective national Hispanic leadership in the US, we may have to wait till the 1990s. But the statistics bespeak the tremendous

[1] Reprint of article entitled "Hispanics in the U.S.: Ethnic 'Sleeping Giant' Awakens," by Geoffrey Godsell, staff correspondent. *The Christian Science Monitor.* p 3. Ap. 28, '80. Reprinted by permission from *The Christian Science Monitor.* © 1980 The Christian Science Publishing Society. All rights reserved.

likely impact on the country when this eventually comes about.

By the end of the century, Hispanics will almost certainly overtake blacks to become the biggest minority in the land. The Bureau of the Census estimated there were 12,046,000 Hispanics in the US in March 1978. That was 5.6 percent of the total population, compared with 11.6 percent for blacks. Leo Estrada of the Chicano Studies Center at the University of California at Los Angeles says the figure for Hispanics "represents the minimum level of Latino population . . . the lowest responsible estimate." These 1978 figures may well have to be revised significantly upward when the results of this April's census are tabulated.

Add to the Bureau of the Census 1978 total the estimated 7.4 million Hispanics in the US illegally (or "undocumented" in the preferred description of Spanish-speakers) and the percentage of the whole becomes 9.1. If one wants to recognize how rapidly and steeply the curve on the graph will rise, a couple of other facts must be stated. First, the birthrate of Hispanics in the US is more than twice that of whites and 60 percent higher than that of blacks. Second, Hispanic immigration into the US, mostly Mexican, is running about 1 million a year—if one includes the illegal with the legal arrivals.

The head of the Roman Catholic Church's Southeastern regional office for Hispanics in Miami, the Rev. Mario Vizcaino, brings home the point of the size of the Hispanic population in this country in an unconventional way. He argues that the US is the fifth-largest Hispanic country in the world, in terms of population, after Mexico, Spain, Argentina, and Colombia.

Mexicans and North Americans

But the challenge lies not only in numbers. It involves also the digesting into the US mainstream of a vast segment of the population much of which sees itself as both linguistically and culturally different. This raises in turn the question: Can it be done without disruptive collision or confrontation?

In one of his perceptive essays, Octavio Paz has written of the differences, as he sees them, between North Americans and Mexicans—who, it should be remembered, constitute some 60 percent of all Hispanics in the US.

> The North Americans . . . love fairy tales and detective stories and we love myths and legends. . . . North Americans want to understand and we want to contemplate. They are activists and we are quietists; we enjoy our wounds and they enjoy their inventions. They believe in hygiene, health, work, and contentment, but perhaps they have never experienced true joy, which is an intoxication, a whirlwind. In the hubbub of a fiesta night our voices explode into brilliant lights, and life and death mingle together, while their vitality becomes a fixed smile that denies old age and death but that changes life to motionless stone.

(Elsewhere in the essay, Mr. Paz writes of the Mexican's "willingness to contemplate horror" and of his "cult of death.")

Some may find Mr. Paz's identification of the basic difference between the two cultures overstark. Yet he has zeroed in on the dividing line between them.

His description of mainstream citizens of the US as "North Americans" is worth noting. That is how most Hispanics in this hemisphere describe their English-speaking neighbors to the north. To Hispanics, the term "Americans" without any qualification (such as "Latin," "South," or Central) means themselves.

At the same time, "Hispanic" does not come naturally to their lips to describe themselves. Mario Barrera, coordinator of Chicano studies at the University of California at Berkeley, said many younger Hispanics deliberately avoid the word because they see it as an English invention foisted on them. This writer found many Hispanics of all ages across the country favoring the word "Latino" when they needed an umbrella description for all Spanish-speakers in the US. But when they were speaking specifically about themselves, they simply said "Mexican," "Puerto Rican," or "Cuban"—as the case might be.

Then there is the word "Anglo," used loosely by Hispanics

to describe anybody or anything in the US that is not Hispanic. Purists might insist that "Anglo" means anything not
Hispanic and not identified with another US minority. But
the Rev. Pedro Villaroya of the Church of Our Lady of Talpa
in East Los Angeles described blacks as "Anglo"—reminding
this writer of black sociologist E. Franklin Frazier's designa-
tion of blacks as "exaggerated Americans."

Before leaving terminology, there are two other words
often used by Mexican-Americans that deserve comment—
not least because of their emotional content. One is "Chicano" (already appearing twice in this article). The other is
"la raza." "Chicano" is synonymous with "Mexican-American" and is apparently a folk abbreviation of "Mexicano," in
the Spanish pronunciation of which the "x" is approximately
like the "ch" in the Scottish "loch."

Where Hispanics Live

Now to return to the wide sweep of Hispanics. How are
they divided up and where in the US do they live? Figure I
shows the relative proportions of Mexicans, Puerto Ricans,
Cubans, and Central or South American or other Spanish origin. Figure II gives the percent distribution of all these by residence. Figure III lists the 10 cities in the US with the biggest
Hispanic populations.

Of these cities, Los Angeles belongs (in Hispanic eyes) to
the Mexicans, New York to the Puerto Ricans, and Miami to
the Cubans. Chicago is unique in that it is the only big city in
the US whose Hispanic population is shared by Mexicans,
Puerto Ricans, and Cubans roughly in the same proportion as
they share the total Hispanic population of the US. San Francisco and Washington (the latter not in the top 10) have un-
usual concentrations of Hispanics from Central and South
America. The seeds for this Washington concentration were
in great measure planted by domestic staff originally intro-
duced by Latin American diplomatic missions. These domestics then found ways of subsequently bringing in often equally
impoverished family members from their home countries.

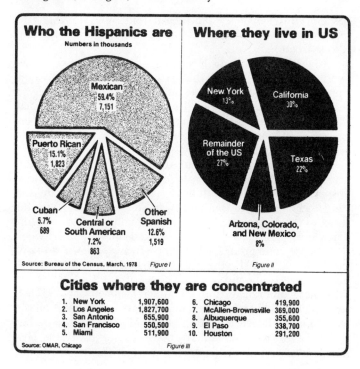

Who the Hispanics are
Numbers in thousands

Mexican
59.4%
7,151

Puerto Rican
15.1%
1,823

Cuban
5.7%
689

Central or
South American
7.2%
863

Other
Spanish
12.6%
1,519

Source: Bureau of the Census, March, 1978   *Figure I*

Where they live in US

New York
13%

California
30%

Remainder
of the US
27%

Texas
22%

Arizona, Colorado,
and New Mexico
8%

Figure II

Cities where they are concentrated

1.	New York	1,907,600	6.	Chicago	419,900
2.	Los Angeles	1,827,700	7.	McAllen-Brownsville	369,000
3.	San Antonio	655,900	8.	Albuquerque	355,600
4.	San Francisco	550,500	9.	El Paso	338,700
5.	Miami	511,900	10.	Houston	291,200

Source: OMAR, Chicago   *Figure III*

Five Southwestern states once part of Mexico have always had heavy Hispanic (and specifically Mexican) populations: California, Texas, Arizona, New Mexico, and Colorado. Today, more and more Mexicans are moving out and away from this traditional area. Leo Estrada says: "Most of these people are going to the Midwest, specifically Illinois, Wisconsin, Missouri, Kansas, etc. It's a still unrecognized fact that Ohio and Minnesota have as many Mexican Americans as Colorado and Nevada." (*Nuestro* magazine, September, 1979)

Illinois and Florida have bigger Hispanic populations than most other non-Southwestern states, based on the urban concentrations already mentioned in Chicago and Miami. While the Puerto Rican presence, based on New York City, has moved out over the Northeast from New York State to Pennsylvania, New Jersey, Connecticut, Massachusetts, and Rhode Island.

Anglo perceptions of Hispanics are often colored by an overall stereotype image that Hispanics themselves understandably resent and consider unfair. Most objectionable to them is the widespread belief in the rest of US society that they are lazy, spongers, and prone to gang activity. The stereotype is, of course, as misleading in their case as in that of any other group or nationality.

Another distorting factor in Anglos' perception of Hispanics is the limitation of regional experience. In other words, Hispanics mean different things to Anglos in different areas of the US. For those in the Southwest, it means Mexicans, for those in the Northeast, Puerto Ricans, and for those in Florida, Cubans. In fact, there are marked differences between these three main groups. Marcelino Miyares, the Cuban-born president of OMAR, the Chicago-based biggest Hispanic-owned advertising and research concern in the US, has gone into these differences and identified many of them. (They tend, incidentally, to set the Cubans apart somewhat from the Mexicans and Puerto Ricans.) But Mr. Miyares concludes that the three groups "are similar enough . . . to justify the Hispanic-American concept."

THE MEXICAN AMERICANS: A PEOPLE ON THE MOVE[2]

Among the 7.3 million Mexican Americans are a number . . . [of successful entrepreneurs like] Tony Sanchez of Laredo, for example, who struck it rich in petroleum leases. And there are other achievers like Bernie Hernandez of San Diego and Al Juárez of Los Angeles, who in the white-collar professional

    [2] Excerpts from article by Griffin Smith, Jr., free-lance writer. *National Geographic.* 157:780-91. Je. '80. Copyright © 1980 by National Geographic Society. Reprinted by permission.

world have built comfortable livings far beyond their child-
hood dreams. There are those, too, like Rocendo Hernandez,
a farm worker, whose life follows the harvests, and George,
just George, who spent his boyhood in the endless gang warfare of the barrio and, when I met him, was soon to die, by the
gun, at 16.

And finally, there are the border crossers, who dash across
from Mexico for work, for a better life, perhaps hoping someday to become Mexican Americans themselves.

Mexican Americans are as diverse as America. Their median family income is $12,570 a year—well under the na-
tional average of $17,640—and about 20 percent fall below
the government-drawn poverty line. Most live in cities instead of on farms, as commonly thought. On the whole they
come from larger families and have higher birthrates and less
education than Caucasians or blacks.

Although nine out of ten Mexican Americans live in the
four southwestern border states, regional differences there are
vivid. Texas sustains a deeper, older, more homogeneous
Mexican-American culture than California. In Arizona the
Indian presence is strongly felt; tribes like the mysterious
Yaqui exist on the periphery of Mexican-American life. In
New Mexico a growing Chicano consciousness is making in-
roads even among the aloof descendants of Spanish colonial
settlers who have preserved a separate existence for centuries
in the mountains north of Santa Fe.

Too little known, Mexican Americans also are too often
misunderstood. But that is changing. In a decade they have
become a phenomenon to be reckoned with. As their numbers
swell and their ethnic awareness grows, they are transforming
much of the U.S. Southwest into Mexico U.S.A. . . .

Heritage and History

Most Mexican Americans would agree that the Roman
Catholic religion, the Spanish language, and a close family
life are basic. Some say the Mexican-American family is a
sanctuary against the world. It is undoubtedly a circle of deep

affection—within a rigid order. The father is the unchallenged master, the mother is guide and nurturer of the children. . . .

Mexican Americans are a people in transition. They are concerned not only with upward mobility and economic success, but also with the acceptance of their ancestral language and traditions in an America that has not always received them gladly. They are energetically surveying their distinctive contributions to the nation's life and embarking on a quest for self-definition. The days of being slightly ashamed of things Mexican are past. . . .

When the Treaty of Guadalupe Hidalgo ended the war between Mexico and the United States in 1848, some 75,000 Mexican citizens were living in the vast southwestern area that became United States territory. The American settlers who claimed the plains and deserts all the way to California were joined occasionally by Mexican pioneers. . . . But . . . [these] were the exception until 1910, when revolutionary fervor in Mexico produced a wave of refugees seeking asylum.

In 1924 the number of immigrants rose to 100,000. After World War II far greater numbers came seeking jobs and opportunity. The 1970s experienced a torrent of illegal immigrants that shows no sign of abating.

For Mexican Americans the recent influx has been both a problem and a source of pride. Unlike the much earlier tide of emigrants from many European countries, the new arrivals from Mexico reflected its mestizo heritage: Indian in "blood and soul," Spanish in "language and civilization." And—again unlike those from Europe—they did not separate themselves by an ocean from their old homeland. Mexico was still just across a river or a line in the desert. The proximity of friends and family helped preserve a bond that emigrants from more distant places lost.

[For further discussion of the Chicano ethnic and cultural identity within the larger community, see "The Chicano Subculture and the Anglo Mainstream," in Section III, below.—Ed.]

THE LATINIZATION OF MIAMI[3]

"The capital of Latin America" is what President Jaime
Roldós of Ecuador dubbed Miami last year during an address
to a group of hemispheric businessmen and bankers. If his re-
mark was somewhat extravagant, it was also within reason,
for if any one city qualifies for the title, it is Miami, with an
annual Trade Fair of the Americas that this year registered
$67.8 million in sales; a newly formed free trade zone that
does an average of $10 million worth of business monthly, and
a financial community that includes more out-of-state and international banks than any other city in the country save New
York. The one-time winter vacation destination of the East
Coast is now the nexus of trade that extends through all of
Central and South America and much of the Caribbean. And
even the most conservative Miamians admit that they owe it
all to Fidel Castro, for it is an article of faith in Miami that
without the impetus provided by the Cuban-exile community
the city today would be just another Sun Belt spa well past its
prime.

But if Miami has become a financial heaven for Latin
Americans, it has also become an economic hell for its own
blacks and a pressure cooker of resentments for Anglo Miamians. (In Miami, if you are not Cuban and not black, you
are, by local definition, an Anglo.)

Miami blacks are desperate and angry. They see a black
unemployment rate of 9.3 percent, a paucity of black-owned
businesses, substandard black housing, and they distrust the
criminal-justice system—elements of which contributed to
the bloody May riot that shocked the community and the rest
of the country. Not an uncommon set of grievances for an
urban black community, but Miami's blacks also see themselves as unwitting victims of the Latinization of their city.

[3] Excerpts from article by Herbert Burkholz, a New York-based journalist and nov-
elist. New York Times *Magazine.* p 44–7+. S. 21, '80. © 1980 by The New York Times
Company. Reprinted by permission.

Anglo Community Resentments

The resentments that simmer within the Anglo community are more subtle. Along with the blacks, white Miamians resent the concentration of financial power achieved by the Cuban exiles, and, equally, they resent the introduction of another language and another culture into a way of life that was, until recently, a combination of Southern and Northern roots. Unwilling to participate in what they now regard as the inevitable Latinization of Miami, many Anglos are responding to the most recent influx of Cuban immigrants with a corresponding exodus of their own to other parts of Florida.

The Miami they are leaving evolved into a center of Latin-American commerce through a combination of coincidence and diligence that began 20 years ago when the first wave of Cuban refugees arrived shortly after Fidel Castro took over in Havana. At that time, the City of Miami lived in the shadow of its more glamorous neighbor across Biscayne Bay, the winter resort of Miami Beach. More than water separated the two. Miami Beach was an internationally famous playground, while Miami itself had little that was glamorous about it. Nestled between the bay and the Everglades swamps, it was the home of the people, mostly of Southern heritage and folkways, who ran the local government or worked in the resort hotels. By the time of Castro's takeover, Miami Beach had already seen its heyday as a resort, and Miami's downtown was deteriorating as the stores followed residents into suburbs that were reclaiming swampland. The first of the refugees received substantial aid from the Federal Government to help in their resettlement, and much of this money was invested directly in Miami's downtown area, and the old, somnolent Cuban-American community suddenly erupted into a new economic activity to meet the housing and job needs of the newcomers. This first wave of refugees contained a disproportionately large number of professionals (not only doctors and lawyers, but engineers, designers, publishers, accountants, manufacturers and importers), a natural result of the Communist overthrow of the Cuban establishment, who created a boom of their own through a series of economic ventures based on their special knowledge and expertise.

A Major Economic Base

Almost inevitably, these twin triumphs attracted investors from other Latin-American countries impressed by the success of the Cuban refugees, and who felt more at ease in the Hispanic ambiance of Miami than in New York, or in any other major trade center. Businessmen as diverse as Argentine ranchers, Ecuadorean manufacturers and Colombian drug peddlers made their way north to do business, and once they had established Miami as a major economic base it followed that they, and other Latin-American businessmen, would also begin to use the city as a vacation spot for themselves and their families. With this, the transformation was complete, and Miami entered the 1980s as a bilingual and bicultural community, not with the cosmetic patina of a Texas border town or the pocket-ghetto vibrancy of the Puerto Rican *barrio* in New York, but with the cosmopolitanism of a major economic center for the more than 342 million people of Latin America.

"Miami would not be what it is, or where it is, if it were not for the Cuban community," says Mayor Maurice Ferré, a man of Puerto Rican origin who has been the city's Mayor since 1973. Ferré considers the bustling aggressiveness of Cubans unique in Latin American society. "Most Hispanic communities have this ability to take abuse passively," he says. "They're not very demanding and they're happy with very little. But not the Cubans. They're extremely competitive, they're extremely aggressive. Not only do they want the best, they want it first."

Cubans, long before Castro, had admired American business practices as well as much of its neighbor's popular culture. Many of the exiles who arrived in Florida had been educated in American schools or already had business connections on the continent.

In describing Miami today, Ferré compares it to Beirut in pre-civil war Lebanon: a cultural, financial and recreational center designed for a specific ethnic group, regardless of national boundaries. "A self-respecting Arab businessman, no matter where he lived, would keep a bank account in Beirut. He'd also have a little apartment there, where he could visit with his girlfriend or take his family and, eventually, his kids would go to the American or the French University there. . . ."

If Miami is not yet as Spanish as Lima or Caracas, it is making strides in that direction. In 20 years, the Hispanic community has grown from 6 percent of the population of the Greater Miami area to 41 percent, only barely a minority, and shows no signs of stopping. Miami is no longer a bilingual city in which Spanish is a handy second language to have. Spanish comes first in many parts of Miami today, and, from a business viewpoint, anyone who doesn't have a working acquaintance with the language, or access to Spanish-speaking personnel, is at a competitive disadvantage.

This rampant Hispanicism pleases Ferré on two levels. As a man of Hispanic background himself, he sees it as an important cultural infusion into American life and, as the Mayor of "the capital of Latin America," he considers it an invaluable selling tool. Continuing his Beirut analogy, Ferré ticks off points on his fingers.

The situation here is even better than it was in Beirut. Because in Miami you have the American flag, the American Constitution, American laws, American products, the American economic structure . . . and all in Spanish. You can come here and buy a computer, an airplane, a house or an apartment; you can invest in the stock market or buy United States bonds . . . and all in Spanish. What you have in Miami is a total infrastructure that's unique in the American experience.

What is also unique to the commerce of the city is the unprecedented amounts of money deposited in, or laundered through, Miami banks as a direct result of the drug trade from the Caribbean and South America, particularly from Colombia. In fact, according to law-enforcement authorities, at least four banks in the area are actually owned by drug dealers. The drug trade is an accepted fact of economic life, and stories abound of "Colombian cowboys" walking around with huge sums of cash in wicker suitcases, asking directions to the nearest bank.

Ferré deplores the drug trade from a moral point of view, calling it "terrible, a depravity of the human soul." But he also concedes that "from an economic point of view, once that money goes into the bank and gets deposited, and is loaned out to build more condominiums ... well, money is money." ...

Culture and Language

Many members of the Anglo community are dismayed to see that parts of Coral Gables, Southwest Miami and most of Hialeah are now exclusively Cuban. They see the Tamiami Trail leading out of the city as five miles of occupied territory filled with restaurants where they would be hard put to order a meal and shopping centers where English is rarely spoken. They see that the parks of Key Biscayne, once their own wonderland of picnic grounds and beaches, are now awash in a sea of strange tongues. They see almost 10,000 Cuban-owned businesses where, 10 years ago, there were less than 1,000. All about them, an alien culture is flourishing on American soil, and many of them echo a local housewife when she says, "Everything has to be bilingual, bilingual, bilingual. Enough is enough." [A referendum barring Dade County from utilizing any language other than English in official transactions was voted into law in November 1980.—Ed.]

That this resentful attitude toward the Cuban community is a relatively new phenomenon was indicated recently in a poll taken by the Miami *Herald.* The newspaper asked its readers whether they thought the new wave of 118,000 Cuban immigrants (an estimated 60,000 of whom have stayed on in Dade County) would have a positive or a negative effect on the area, 17 percent of the Anglo readers responded positively and 68 percent negatively, with the rest undecided; the black response was 16 percent positive, 57 percent negative. But when the same question was asked about the previous waves of Cuban immigrants—the 400,000 who have transformed and revitalized the city—50 percent of the Anglos responded positively and only 29 percent responded negatively, while the figures for black reader response were 48 percent positive and 45 percent negative.

This marked division between "old" and "new" Cubans in the minds of the Anglos of Miami has created a tension of its own. Marvin Dunn, a professor of psychology at Florida International University, admits that "the community is schizo. Our ideals conflict with the practical task of trying to live. It's very difficult to put these things together, and we're in for an intense period of interethnic and intercultural conflict."

Black Leadership in Miami

The riot this May in the heavily black Liberty City area of Miami began as a protest against the acquittal of four white policemen charged with the fatal beating of Arthur McDuffie, a black Miami insurance executive. (The policemen are now the subject of an investigation by a Federal grand jury.) But no one doubts that the McDuffie case was only the spark that ignited some highly combustible tinder that had been piling up for a long time. "There is no question," says Mayor Ferré, "that poverty, lack of jobs, rats, people sleeping 10 to an apartment and child abuse were underlying reasons."

Leaders of Miami's black community, while agreeing with the Mayor's assessment, add that the already sensitive situation has been highly inflamed by the most recent wave of Cuban immigration. . . .

"They bring everybody to Miami," says one black resident of the ravaged Liberty City area. "Nicaraguans, Cubans, Haitians. And we're still on the bottom. We can't even get to the first step to make it to the top."

The inability to reach this first step reflects the lack of political power and the low level of leadership in black Miami. One reason is that the history of Miami's black community is relatively short, going back only as far as the 1920s, when the resort boom made the area a winter haven for Easterners. It was only then that blacks from neighboring Georgia and Alabama began to arrive in Miami in substantial numbers to work in the newly erected hotels in Miami Beach. Since then, the black community has been augmented by arrivals from all over the Southeast, but the absence, until very recently, of an industrial economy has meant that black incomes have remained tied to the unskilled labor market or the semiskills of a service industry. The result, says Athalie Range, who was Miami's first black City Commissioner, is a "rootless" community that has been able to exert very little control over its own destiny. . . .

With its population swollen to 1.7 million by the new Cuban refugees, the city has to find 60,000 new jobs this year and no one is confident that the black community will get its share. The prevailing feeling is that many Cuban businessmen will create jobs for Cuban refugees, not because of a need for additional labor but out of a sense of Hispanic solidarity and family ties. Employment and welfare lines will, therefore, probably continue to be predominantly black.

Economic Aid Programs

Black Miami has received promises of aid, large and small from the state and Federal Governments, but State Representative [Carrie] Meek characterizes the state's offer as "much too little." The Federal package, also denounced as inadequate by Senator Lawton Chiles, Democrat of Florida, is an amalgam of programs totaling $90 million in aid, including loans to rebuild businesses, economic development, job training, improved security in public housing, rapid-transit construction and health care in the riot area. According to Senator Chiles, the aid program had already been planned and would have been granted whether the riot occurred or not. Only recently has some money—$20 million of it—begun to trickle down to the community. . . .

While both the state and Federal aid packages have been

branded inadequate, the mood in the Florida legislature
seems to be that black Miami will have to dig its way out of
its rubble with the money it's already been offered. Summing
up this attitude, State Representative Barry Kutun, Democrat
of Dade County, says, "In no way will legislation be passed
that will be a reward for rioting." . . .

The Dade County Department of Public Safety, like the
Miami Police Department, has relatively few blacks on its
rolls, and a recent survey by the United States Commission on
Civil Rights reports that the proportion of black male officers
has actually declined in the last five years from 6.3 percent to
5.5 percent. In the aftermath of the rioting, however, both
the city and county police departments have announced
plans to hire 200 more officers, of whom 60 percent will be
black, Hispanic or female. Despite this promise, black Miami
still looks askance at a criminal justice system in which there
are wide disparities between the sentences given to whites
and to blacks, and in which relatively few black state attor-
neys and public defenders are employed.

Is there, then, a future for the black community in the
capital of Latin America? Blacks insist that there has to be. "I
don't believe that blacks here will ever be apathetic again,"
says Carrie Meek. Anglo and Cuban leaders publicly support
this insistence, but privately they admit that the odds are very
long. They also admit, privately, that they wish the problem
would simply disappear. The union of Anglo finance and
Cuban hustle is more than a marriage of convenience. It is a
marriage that was made in a commercial heaven, and neither
the bride nor the groom has a profound desire to deal with the
problems of a stepchild who happens to be black.

Blacks and Refugees

Everyone agrees that something must be done to improve
the economic position of the black community. The need is
urgent, and not only because of the mood of the people.
While many of the first wave of refugees were professionals
who quickly progressed from menial jobs to better paying po-

sitions, almost all of the recent refugees are unskilled workers who will for some time continue to stand between blacks and the few jobs available. Sensing the explosive potential in the situation, a Cuban banker and community leader by the name of Carlos Arboleya launched a campaign to provide assistance to the unemployed new immigrants. His message to Cuban businessmen was uncompromisingly direct: "Each Cuban adopt a Cuban. Let's help. Let's counsel. Let's guide them." It also meant: Let's hire them.

When the boat lift of Cubans from Mariel Harbor to Key West began last April, the burden of handling the refugees fell in great measure on Metropolitan Dade County. Paul Reingold, an executive assistant to County Mayor Stephen P. Clark and one of those closely involved with caring for the refugees when they first arrived, still expresses resentment at the way the Federal Government dealt with the situation.

"The Federal people in Key West simply took the names of the refugees and told them to make their way to Miami," he says. "We were being flooded here, but for eight days Washington refused to acknowledge that the Cubans were coming in. Eventually, we had a lot of high-level people come down here, but all they could say was, 'Yes, you've got a problem.' Our position was that we couldn't quite see how immigration was a county problem. But the simple fact of the matter was that these people had to be housed, had to be fed, and they couldn't be allowed to roam the streets." . . .

Miami and Latin American Commerce

What Reingold does is put Latin American businessmen and investors in touch with American banks, whose borrowing rates are considerably more advantageous than in inflation-ravaged Central and South America. With the interest rate for top-line companies now pegged at 24 percent in Venezuela, 28 percent in Chile and a whopping 42 percent (with a floating index) in Brazil, the American market has become highly attractive to investors from these countries, and to most of them the American market means Miami. "Financing is so cheap here by their standards that it's ridiculous," says Reingold. . . .

Like almost every other successful businessman in Miami today, Reingold has learned to speak Spanish and to adjust to the Latin style of doing business, although at times he seems mildly exasperated by the process. "We've got a shopping center going up on Sunset and 117th, a substantial investment, being built with Colombian money. Well, I went down to Colombia five or six times. I took plans, I took architects, charts, cash flows—you name it. These guys were resisting all the way. Then I brought them up here. They walked on the land, the actual land, and we closed the deal the same day. Latins like to sink their money into things they can touch. Because of the political atmosphere in much of Latin America, things are pretty iffy and you could have something today and it could be gone tomorrow. So I've learned. Get them here and show them around, even if there's nothing on the property right now."

While black Miami sweltered through the tensions of a long, hot summer and while Anglo Miami nervously consulted road maps and job offers in Rochester, N.Y., and Tucson, Ariz., the Cuban community prepared to mark the culmination of 20 years of entrepreneurial triumph.

"God gave Miami the geographical location," says Evelio Ley, a prominent Cuban-American businessman, "and Castro gave Miami an excellent Cuban community. In return, Anglo-Saxon Miami made us welcome and gave us protection. That was all we needed."

If there is a single symbol that represents Miami's newly acquired role in Latin American commerce, it is the annual Trade Fair of the Americas, of which Ley is the prime mover and promoter. Ley is a typical Cuban success story, rags to riches in less than 20 years. He arrived in Miami on July 4, 1961, with $20 in his pocket and a few words of phrase-book English on his lips. These days, he not only promotes the trade fair but also spends a considerable part of each year traveling throughout Latin America as Miami's unofficial drum beater and apologist. Speaking of the rioting this summer, he says: "The first reaction in Latin America was very negative. The people there were afraid to do business with us and we have to reassure them." . . .

A Role for Blacks

Evelio Ley is one of those who admits that "there is a role for the black people to play in Miami." But, he says, "I have to tell you that I don't think that role has been properly exploited up to now." He goes on to envision an African Trade Fair modeled along the lines of his Trade Fair of the Americas. In his conception of the African version, the black community would take the lead in fostering commercial exchanges between African nations and American suppliers and distributors through an exhibition to be held annually in Miami. He concedes, however, that he is only just beginning to explore the possibilities. The suggestion, however earnestly presented, betrays the paucity of thinking that the local community has brought to the postriot period of self-examination. The fact is the Latins, who are assuming power in Miami, have not been predisposed—other than piecemeal efforts—to confront the black problem in significant ways, and have been so preoccupied with their own struggle that they have not yet reached that point of social development when they can take up someone else's cause with the same enthusiasm as their own.

CUBANS IN NEW JERSEY[4]

By the time he was 10 years old, Isidro Ortega Jr., now 22, had learned to reassemble a stripped-down Polish submachine gun, read Marx and had been asked to spy on his family.

Olga Ortega's eyes narrow with rage at what was done to her two sons in the name of the Cuban revolution.

[4] Reprint of article entitled "Slow, Steady Climb up the Ladder," by Donnel Nunes, staff writer. Washington *Post.* p A1+. Jl. 7, '80. © 1980 The Washington Post. Reprinted by permission.

"You know, they used to come into the school and say, 'Children,' close your eyes and pray to God to give you ice cream,'" she recalls. "The children prayed and then they told them to open their eyes and, of course, there was no ice cream.

"Then they said, 'Children, close your eyes and pray to Fidel Castro for ice cream.' So they closed their eyes and when they opened them there was ice cream. 'Now you know who takes care of you,' they said."

She flips through an old family album, one of the few belongings the Ortegas were permitted to take when they fled Cuba in 1968. Past the pictures of her sons in their school uniforms—miniature military fatigues—past the pictures of relatives left behind and relatives now dead, the Havana skyline in the background. Then she shuts it abruptly.

"No," she says, "even if Castro left Cuba today, I could never go back now." Her pained face suddenly brightens. "I'm American. I can't even eat Cuban food anymore."

For the more than 30,000 Cubans in this aging community of 60,000 across the Hudson from the Manhattan skyline [Union City, New Jersey], the bitter memories of what happened in their homeland are slowly fading. They are too preoccupied with making their way in their new land.

But while the longtime residents here see the Cubans as only the latest in the successive waves of immigrants—German, then Irish, then Italian—who first beached in Union City on the way to becoming Americans, the Cubans say their reasons for coming make them unique.

"We didn't come just because there were jobs here," said Ibrael Suarez, 50, who came in 1970. "I had a relatively good job as an agricultural expert. I even had a car for my job. I came because I was not a communist and I wanted to raise my family the way I wanted to raise it, not the way the government wanted me to raise it."

Whatever their reasons for coming, the Cubans have transformed this city.

After Italians, the last immigrants to call it home, moved up the economic ladder and then moved out, the Cubans bought the storefronts left vacant. They put up signs advertising *ropas* (clothes) and *zapatos* (shoes). They worked in factories during the economic boom of the 1960s. They bought homes that had been vacant for years and pushed up property values.

"When they started to come in the 1960s this place was dying," says Galto Serafino, a Union City realtor and native, the son of an Italian immigrant. "There were apartments available, storefronts available. There was room. And we were glad to see them come."

"Now there's not an area you can go to and not find a Cuban," says Jim Lagomarsino, another Italian American raised in Union City. "They'll use this place just like our families did. A steppingstone. A doorstep to America."

The Success of the Cubans

Overall, the Cubans have been remarkably successful.

According to a Cuban Planning Council survey, roughly one out of every five Cuban wage earners here is classified as a professional or manager. The median Cuban family income in this somewhat depressed area is $14,555. While the national unemployment rate is 7.7 percent and the local rate is nearly 10 percent, only 6.7 percent of the Cubans here are unemployed.

Proportionately fewer Cubans are on welfare than members of other ethnic groups. They pay taxes on time, giving Union City one of the highest collection rates of return in the area. And they look after their own by contributing thousands of dollars toward the resettlement of new refugees and giving them clothing and old furniture to start them off.

Some Cubans, who apparently had connections with organized crime in the old pre-Castro Cuba, are reportedly using Union City as a distribution center for narcotics coming from Miami, police say.

"There have been a few involved in heroin traffic," said Capt. George Yannuzzi. "But we think they're hangovers from the old days when the Mafia was thinking of making

Havana the gambling capital of the world. There are bad ones in any lot."

Police in Union City are quick to point out that only a handful of the Cubans has ever been suspected of having any connection with the drug trade.

Part of the economic success is attributable to the sheer numbers of Cubans who have come to the United States and Union City in the last 20 years—at least 855,000 nationally, not including the 117,000 who came by boat earlier this year. The large Cuban communities that resulted softened the cultural shock many new arrivals might otherwise have experienced.

At the same time, the strong cultural and business ties Cuba had over the years with the United States have given most Cubans an insight into American viewpoints, an adjustment asset that most other immigrants and refugees lack.

Yet there are problems. Many older Cubans have great difficulty in learning English, a handicap that keeps them rooted in low-paying blue-collar jobs where there are large numbers of other Spanish-speakers. The resulting isolation causes problems, but because of pride, few take advantage of mental health services.

The nation's economic ills are affecting the Cubans, too. Those who don't speak English cannot find new jobs easily. The community—both Cuban and non-Cuban—is also nervous about the possible impact on the job market of the 10,-000 to 12,000 new Cuban refugees expected to settle in Union City in the next few months.

The increased competition for jobs also worries some who fear that it will prompt an increase in latent anti-Cuban sentiment felt by a few longtime residents and the growing number of Puerto Ricans in the area, who also are affected by the nation's economic woes.

"You've got to be Spanish-speaking to get a job," said Billy Metzner, 24, a mechanic whose family came as German immigrants to Union City. "The Cubans, they come over, they get everything. We Americans don't get nothing. The companies would rather have the Spanish working for them because they work for peanuts."

There is no denying the overwhelming Cuban presence in the community. The language on the streets is Spanish. Stores advertise their goods in Spanish, a few noting in their windows: "English spoken here." Even the menus in Chinese restaurants are in Spanish, and the Chinese owners speak Spanish far more easily than English.

It is within this tightly knit ethnic community, reminiscent of the Little Italys and Irelands of the past, that families like the Ortegas and Suarezes are steadily climbing upward. But it has not been easy.

When Ibrael Suarez brought his mother and father, his wife and three daughters to Union City from Camaguey, Cuba, he was penniless. His lack of English, plus his lack of documents attesting to his education in agriculture (the Cuban government refused to let him take them with him) left him no choice but factory work.

Like most of the Cubans here, he came because friends and family had come before him. With their help, he rented a small apartment for $150 a month, took a $110-a-week job, and began the time-honored economic climb of the immigrant.

Today he earns about $240 a week working for a wire company. He has a 4-year-old son, born in America, and his daughters are graduating from high school with thoughts of going to college. He has recently moved to the suburbs to rent a house owned by his brother who once lived in Union City himself.

"There are things I have learned," he says. "Happiness is not here anymore than anywhere else. It is not all like we Cubans would have wanted it to be. Yet, we have everything we need. We live, practically speaking, well. We economize so the children can get a good education. The American dream exists. We can live happily. There is work."

The Ortegas are on their way up, too. When Olga and her husband Isidro Ortega came to Union City a dozen years ago from Spain, the only country to which the Cuban government would allow them to emigrate, they had $5 and some family photo albums of life in better times in Havana.

Today they own a small frame house in Union City that they bought from another Cuban two years ago for $37,000, using money they had saved diligently for years. "I think it is worth about $6,000 more today," said Mrs. Ortega proudly.

They give clothing and old furniture to the new crop of Cuban refugees, just as more established Cuban families offered them hand-me-downs when they first came.

Isidro Ortega was a traffic policeman in Batista's government when Castro came to power. It was a black mark against him. Mrs. Ortega worked for a novelty store that sold items to American tourists. That also made her suspect in the communist government's eyes. After Castro solidified his power, she was thrown out of work and never permitted to hold a job again, while her husband was forced to work as a cab driver, using the old American car he had purchased before the revolution.

But his policeman past caught up with him, and the government sent him to a forced labor farm camp for 14 months.

When the Ortegas finally arrived in Union City—a cousin was here already, providing them with a tie to the community—Ortega went to work for a chemical company. Mrs. Ortega went to work for a cosmetics firm. Within six months they had saved enough to open a small restaurant in Union City, but the work proved too hard and they sold it a few months later.

"I was making about $1.65 an hour when we first came, and my husband was earning about $2.30 an hour," she said. "So we earned about $160 a week between us. We rented a little apartment here for about $135, spent about $37 a week on food, and felt good."

Eight months after they came, they had also saved enough to buy a $200 used car that they kept for just over two years. Mrs. Ortega went to work for a small baby toy company called Danara Inc., where her two sons now work as well, and her husband found a job in another factory.

Today they own a 1972 compact car they bought a year and a half ago—"it gets better gas mileage," explained Mrs. Ortega—a house that has an apartment they rent to another Cuban family, and they earn about $530 a week between them. Their two sons live at home and contribute $50 each a week toward household food and expenses.

Comparing Cubans and Europeans

The Ortegas and Suarezes are fairly typical of the success and social circumstances of Cubans in the United States, according to studies done by Prof. Barry Chiswick of the University of Chicago, and Prof. Alejandro Portes of Duke University.

According to Chiswick, who compared Cubans to European immigrants, the Cubans start on lower rungs of the economic ladder than do the Europeans. But after about 10 to 13 years, their earnings equal or begin to exceed the earnings of the Europeans.

Portes found, in a study of Cubans who came to Miami in 1972 and 1973, that unemployment is extremely low—4.4 percent as of 1979. At the same time, 40 percent of the sample work either for Cuban-owned businesses or are self-employed.

"They have an overwhelmingly positive attitude toward . . . the United States," he said. "Their original gratitude has not given way to skepticism." He said that the Cubans' success is deeply rooted in the Cuban community, and few, as a result, speak English well.

"An entire life can be conducted within the bounds of that enclave," he said.

Isidro Ortega Jr. is convinced that his family is making the kind of progress that they should, though he feels the older generation sticks together much too much and spends too little time learning English.

"We subscribe to three papers," he said. "I read the New York *Times* and sometimes the Hudson *Dispatch*. My father still reads just *El Diario* (a Spanish language paper) because he doesn't speak enough English."

He smiled. "Someday," he said, "I'll get him to start reading the *Times.*"

CAPE VERDEAN MIGRANTS[5]

They came to this country from a miniature melting pot of their own—the descendants of white Portuguese and black Africans. Theirs is an ethnic tapestry shot through with threads from the Chinese, the Jews, the Moors, the Indians. [Cape Verde, a former Portuguese territory, became independent in 1975.—Ed.]

For the 300,000 Cape Verdeans in the United States— nearly as many as in the Cape Verde Islands—the age-old question of identity is particularly profound.

"My children never knew they were black until they went outside the neighborhood," said Donna Cruz, a waitress in the historical waterfront section of this former whaling capital [New Bedford, Massachusetts]. "The way I was brought up, you'd never say you were black. You were Portuguese. You didn't hang around with Negroes. . . . Now we're taught to have pride."

Cruz is a Cape Verdean-American, one of the thousands who have emigrated to the United States over the last century to escape the perpetual poverty of their drought-swept island country off the west coast of Africa. They refer to their exodus as the only large-scale "voluntary," or non-slave, emigration from Africa.

Southwest of the waterfront here in the shelter of the stone hurricane wall, an immigrant such as Millie Pina, who arrived here three weeks ago, finds familiar terrain. It is the

[5] Reprint of article entitled "Cape Verdeans Face Identity Problems in U.S.," by Kathy Sawyer, staff writer. Washington *Post.* p A1+. Jl. 6, '80. © 1980 The Washington Post. Reprinted by permission.

"second home" she has read about and seen in photographs all her life.

Stretching along both sides of Akushnet Avenue, about 12,000 Cape Verdeans live in a neighborhood of clapboard and shingle homes and blocks of public housing. Jukeboxes in bars feature Cape Verdean "mornas," or laments of farewell, and women cook a rice-and-bean dish called jagacida or, in American slang, "jag."

Yet so few Americans know about them that when they venture outside their familiar neighborhoods—here, in Pawtucket, Providence, Boston and a few other places—as Cruz says: "It's very interesting trying to explain who we are and what we are."

"You might say that the Cape Verdeans are the first example of pure racial democracy," said John (Joli) Gonsalves, a leader of New Bedford's Cape Verdean community.

Some of them joke about being "the green people," after the name of their homeland. Their racial makeup, it seems, confounds not only American social conditioning and bureaucratic pigeonholers but also forces Cape Verdeans themselves into odd dilemmas as they face for the first time a system in which people are judged—to a greater or lesser degree—by color.

In keeping with the great paradox of the modern American "melting pot," a contingent of Cape Verdeans traveled from New Bedford to Washington last fall to try to persuade the U.S. Census to give them their own category in the 1980 count. They wanted it based on their ethnic background as Cape Verdeans, not on race.

They won a concession: instructions on the long form only, asking citizens to be specific when they identify their origins and mentioning Cape Verdeans as an example.

Defining Cape Verdeans

But the burden of defining themselves remains with the individual Cape Verdean.

Along "the avenue" (Akushnet was the name of the whaling ship that carried Herman Melville to sea and helped inspire "Moby Dick"), you can hear many variations, usually in good-natured tones, on the color question.

You hear about Cape Verdeans who, regardless of skin color, consider themselves white and will "hit you with rocks" if you consider them otherwise. You hear of the young Cape Verdean doctor who lives in the suburbs of Boston with his white wife and their children, and who comes home alone to visit his dark-skinned relatives.

You hear about the rising generation of Cape Verdeans, many of whom have taken up the banner of black pride, seeking refuge, as their parents often see it, in an unambiguous identity. "They feel left out; they want to belong somewhere," said one mother.

You hear about the tensions between the new arrivals and the "old guard." The newly arrived immigrants, intent on the economics of survival, are sometimes bewildered by the raised ethnic consciousness of their Americanized countrymen. Other new arrivals are disappointed by Americanized Cape Verdeans who have forgotten their native culture altogether.

Occasional outbreaks of gang violence between young blacks and Cape Verdeans occurred until the '60s focused national attention on civil rights issues. Then things began to change.

"We have a lot of the same problems, a lot to talk about over a beer, you know," said one young Cape Verdean, a plant worker, who said he thinks of himself as an Afro-American.

"Being a Cape Verdean is very, very complex," said Deonilda Rosa, an American-born Cape Verdean who works in the New Bedford office of Rep. Gerry E. Studds (D-Mass.) "You can get a different perception from each person you talk to."

At Alfred J. Gomes Elementary, Mary G. Andrade teaches immigrant children who speak Portuguese and their own unwritten dialect Crioulo, about their culture as well as how to speak English as a second language.

She teaches them about both their Portuguese and their black African sides, she said. "I tell them we come in all colors, hair textures. We all have our own characteristics, our blackness, our whiteness, our in-betweenness. . . ."

Anyone asking for unemployment figures or other information learns that Cape Verdeans cause special headaches for local bureaucrats and public officials.

"It's a hell of a mess and there are no simple answers," said William Tansey of the state unemployment compensation office in New Bedford. He ran through a litany of the changing government code system as it might apply to Cape Verdeans: Portuguese/European, black, caucasian, "other than white," and so on.

"I have two Cape Verdeans in my office," he said.

"One has two Cape Verdean parents and calls herself 'nonwhite, minority' and the other has one Cape Verdean parent and one from the Azores. She calls herself 'white.' But there's hardly any difference in the color of their complexions."

There was a time, he sighed, "when 'nonwhite, other' kept everybody happy."

In the days of school desegregation, some recalled the discomfiture of officials who had to go into classrooms and "visually determine" whether their schools were racially balanced. Their difficulties were compounded when some American blacks claimed to be Cape Verdeans.

In the struggle for jobs in the area's factories, fish processing plants and on merchant ships, Costa said, employers tend to lump all black faces together, regardless of what they call themselves.

"Some, such as Polaroid, have good affirmative action programs," he said. "Generally, because of the visibility factor, they see that face and you get the same treatment as any Afro-American, or as a Hispanic. . . . It's difficult for any minority to get into a union."

Generally, Costa said, Cape Verdeans share equally with blacks and other low-income Americans the problems of unemployment, youthful drug addiction, low pay and lack of education. And they count under federal minority hiring requirements.

Some employers reportedly prefer to hire Cape Verdeans over Afro-Americans because they consider them "less black" but they still count under minority requirements. And some employers say they prefer Cape Verdeans because they not only count as minorities, but also are bilingual and can help in dealing with the large Portuguese population in New Bedford and nearby areas.

"That fills two holes, and that is an asset, believe me," said John Fielding of the state employment office.

Cape Verdeans traditionally have provided a cheap and conscientious source of labor for New England. They were highly regarded (but lowly paid) as harpooners, steersmen and general crewmen on the dangerous and dirty whaling ships of the last century. When that work burned out, they became mainstays in the factories and cranberry bogs on Cape Cod.

A Changing Economy

Now, with the exodus of industry to the Sun Belt, jobs are scarce in New Bedford. Immigrants must have a guarantee of livelihood before they can come here, so many are heading for more prosperous areas such as Boston, said Joli Gonsalves, coordinator of community development for the mayor's office. Still, New Bedford, by all accounts, remains a mecca for Cape Verdeans in this country.

"Sometimes they find it's hard to get a job, or they work long, hard hours, or they have to be separated from their families," said teacher Virginia Neves Gonsalves (who is no relative to Joli).

"But even after the shocks, this is still the best land, the land where God walked on with his own two feet."

In the immigrant tradition, New Bedford's Cape Verdean

community is a chain of families putting down roots and then helping relatives to join them.

Edward (Fast Eddy) Fortes has worked on the New Bedford docks for 27 years. He is a cutter at the Aiello Brothers fish processing plant.

His hands are scarred from occasional side swipes with the filet knife he uses to whittle at high speed on a passing parade of flounder, cod and other species of fish brought in by the Portuguese fishing fleet.

Fast Eddy once cut 86 crates of cod in one day—a record for the town. He earned a $1 bonus for every box past the first 16, he beamed, chomping on a cigar.

Fortes has welcomed a dozen of his relatives to the United States and helped them get jobs, partly by virtue of his power as a union leader.

He has also put his two daughters through college. One is a schoolteacher. The other is studying to become "the only Cape Verdean veterinarian in New Bedford," he said proudly.

"We worked hard to get what we got," he said.

The process of starting a new life in the United States begins, for many Cape Verdeans, with an expensive trip from one island to another in the U-shaped archipelago. The U.S. mission is on Praia, but most emigrants are from Brava or Fogo and the waters between the islands are rough. "That alone can cost $300 to $400," an immigration specialist in Studds' office said.

How Many Migrants?

About 1,100 American visas a year, according to State Department figures, are issued in the islands, which became independent from Portugal in 1975. Priority is usually assigned according to how closely related the applicant is to someone in the United States. The wait in the brother/sister category, for instance, is about 14 months.

The immigrants used to come in two-masted schooners or other ships of the packet trade that carried mail, cargo and passengers on often hazardous voyages between New England and Cape Verde (the islanders pronounce Verde to rhyme with bird), some as recently as 1965.

Now they come by air, usually on money borrowed from their families here. Then their first priority is to earn enough to pay it back, the Studds aide said.

Once here, the new immigrants buy homes as fast as they can, by all accounts, often through a two-family arrangement or a consortium of relatives.

Many people who remain behind on the islands live on what is sent them from relatives here, as well as aid from the United States and other countries. Cape Verde, a landscape of volcanic rock and loose soil, is visited regularly by drought. The current one began in 1968.

Because of emigration, Cape Verde is dominated by women and children (half the population is younger than 18) according to a report in the Providence *Journal*. The fledgling government is exploring for water so that corn and other crops can be cultivated, and is making other moves toward development. But, the report said, the process will take at least 20 years.

Amelia Pina, 24, arrived here just three weeks ago from the village of Pai-luis. Her father was already here. One of the first things she did was to start sewing herself a wedding dress.

She had come on what is called a "fiancée visa." In a couple of weeks, she will marry an American-born Cape Verdean she met when he was visiting her island.

Joseph J. Alves Jr., her fiancé, is a systems programmer for Ford Aerospace in nearby Lexington, Mass. She speaks mostly Crioulo, while he is better, though not fluent, in Portuguese. He is teaching her English.

Pina's only difficulty has been understanding the distances of the American landscape. "To her, you can get anywhere in a day, walking or hitching a ride," Alves said. "It was hard to impress on her where Pittsburgh is when I had to go there."

Alves' father, Jose, had come here in 1929 at age 15 and took a job as cook on an oil tanker at $45 a month. He eventually worked his way up to chief steward.

This is a way of life still favored by some young Cape Verdean men steeped in the seafaring tradition, as Alves was by his whaling grandfather. But Cape Verdeans like to point out that their people are farmers at heart, not seafarers.

In any case, Alves said with a chuckle, "The sons of seamen don't want nothing to do with it ..."

"Not my kind of life," said his computer specialist son.

The men are out for months at a time, and although the pay is good (nearly $900 a month for seven months plus a high percentage of full pay for five months off), it gets lonely.

"When you're young, it is a very good life," Alves said. "Fortunately, I marry a girl raised over there and she understood ... But when you get old, you realized what you missed, with the kids and all. I have come to realize what my father went through to support the family."

HAITIAN REFUGEES[6]

On August 19, 1979, the New York *Times* carried a special dispatch from reporter Wayne King in Miami; his report read in part:

A woman and five small children drowned, allegedly forced overboard into 20 feet of dark water by two men smuggling them and others into the country, part of a stream of Haitians fleeing their homeland.

Nine made it to the shore alive. One is missing. The body of 31-year-old Elaine Lorfils washed onto the beach. The bodies of the five children, 4–11 years old, were found bobbing in the sea.

On July 2 of this year, in a class-action suit in Miami Federal District Court, Judge James Lawrence King (no relation to reporter King) ruled that more than 4,000 Haitians seeking asylum in the U.S. had been denied due process of law and

[6] Reprint of article entitled "The Haitian Struggle for Human Rights," by Paul Lehmann, emeritus professor, Union Theological Seminary, and chairman, American Committee for the Protection of Foreign Born. *Christian Century.* 97:941–3. 0. 8, '80. Copyright © 1980 Christian Century Foundation. Reprinted by permission.

equal protection of the laws, and had been victims of "systematic and pervasive" discrimination by immigration authorities who had "prejudged Haitian asylum cases as lacking any merit." Judge King found that the manner in which the Immigration and Naturalization Service (INS) had treated these Haitians "violated the Constitution, the immigration statutes, international agreements, INS regulations and INS operating procedures." And he declared: "It must stop!"

Until it does stop, Dieumerci Lorfils—husband of Elaine and father of the five drowned children—is the silent witness to the almost genocidal inhumanity that characterizes the treatment of the Haitian "boat people" by the present government of the U.S. through its departments of Justice and State.

The reporter and the judge have put before the American people in straightforward terms the tragedy and the hope of the Haitian struggle for human rights. In order to understand and responsibly assess this struggle, a brief review is warranted.

A Struggle for Existence

The present plight of the Haitians began in 1957, when François ("Papa Doc") Duvalier assumed power in Haiti. From then until his death in 1971, he ruled this small Caribbean country with a cruel dictatorial power, torturing political opponents and arbitrarily placing citizens in prison without trial or hearing. As he lay dying in 1971, "Papa Doc" Duvalier, as "President-for-Life," proclaimed his son, Jean Claude ("Baby Doc"), his successor with the same title. The principal instruments of presidential repression and suppression of human rights in Haiti have been and remain the Tontons Macoutes, the dreaded secret police force of the Duvaliers—30,000 strong.

Haiti is as miserable economically as it is politically. Long before the present situation erupted, poverty was notorious. The population is largely peasant, subject to the vagaries of precarious small-farm and village existence. One estimate states that 95 per cent of the population is so engaged; estimates of per-capita income range from $80 to $200 per year. Economic deprivation has contributed to a population mobility which has made the Haitian people the wanderers of the Caribbean. They have provided cheap labor, chiefly for the Dominican Republic and the Bahamas—and on this account they have incurred a double jeopardy. On the one hand, they have endured the humiliating discovery that the attempt to break free of a subsistence level at home serves but to make them victims of exploitation abroad. On the other hand, this same search for a viable economic level of existence has made them victims of the judgment, by their own government as well as foreign ones, that they are economic migrants and in no sense political refugees. Since December 12, 1972, when the first boatload of Haitians arrived in Florida after an 800-mile journey of indescribable torment and danger, this fiction has functioned as the cornerstone of U.S. policy toward the Haitians.

Hostility Instead of Hospitality

From the first, the Nixon, Ford and Carter administrations have treated the Haitians with hostility instead of hospitality. Prejudged to be economic and not political refugees, they were given cursory "interviews" upon their arrival, with no attorney permitted. They were imprisoned, often on a $1,000 bond, and those released were denied work authorization. To date, INS has a backlog of over 10,000 asylum cases. The processing of these applications, coupled with those of the Cubans and the normal workload, has confronted INS with an administrative nightmare.

Even more significant, the Carter administration found itself faced with a rapidly worsening political dilemma. After welcoming Cubans for 20 years, Washington "would find it hard to justify turning away the new refugees. Also, the administration had to treat Haitians just as generously lest it be accused of racial bias against the Haitians, who are black" (New York *Times,* June 21).

As far back as February 1974, a resolution of the Governing Board of the National Council of Churches noted this racial aspect and called attention to its "divisive" potential. More recently, the congressional Black Caucus (with Shirley Chisholm and Walter Fauntroy in the lead), the National Urban League and, above all, Haitian communities and the black community in Florida have been in the forefront of the struggle to win political asylum for the Haitians, as a minimal and just recognition of their human rights. Innumerable religious groups (Protestant, Catholic and Jewish), many labor organizations (including the AFL-CIO Executive Council) and government officials (senators, representatives, the governor of Florida and the mayor of Miami) have joined in supporting asylum. This escalating pressure, along with favorable TV coverage and major newspaper editorials favoring asylum, has eroded the Carter administration's opposition to the recognition of Haitian human rights.

A Government Shift

Finally, on June 20 the administration reversed itself. It linked Cuban and Haitian refugees and granted the Haitians parole "entrant status" for six months, pending congressional approval of permanent residence after two years. The post of U.S. coordinator for refugee affairs, carrying the rank of ambassador, was created, and Victor Palmieri was named its first incumbent. Palmieri declared that further extension of parole would be granted, if needed, until final congressional action is taken. Under the new State Department policy, incorporated in a bill now before Congress, the estimated 25,000–30,000 Haitian "boat people" who are known to have arrived on or before June 19 are to be treated as a group and exempted from having to prove individually that they are unable to return to Haiti because of a "well-founded fear" of political persecution. Should this bill become law, it would constitute a modification of the Refugee Act of 1980, which was passed by the Congress in response to the wholesale admission of refugees as "boat people" from southeast Asia.

The Refugee Act of 1980, however, contains an ominous provision. It stipulates the withdrawal of the president's power to apply "parole asylum status" to groups of applicants by March 17, 1980—a date administratively extended to May 15, 1980, in deference to the immediate circumstances. It cannot be too strongly stressed that this action is a marked repudiation of the power vested in the president by the Protocol Relating to the Status of Refugees, Article 33 of the U.S. Refugee Law. Submitted to the Senate by President Lyndon B. Johnson and passed at his urging on November 1, 1968, the protocol was hailed by Johnson as a comprehensive bill of human rights.

Thus, caught between the Cubans, whom it did not wish to refuse, and the Haitians, whom it did not wish to admit, the government devised the new category of parole "entrant status" as a way of granting temporary refuge to the Haitians without having to determine whether they are political or economic refugees—and without altering its treatment of the Cubans. In conformity with this "entrant status," the Haitians meanwhile would be given employment authorization, as well as access to certain federal benefits such as supplementary security income, Medicaid, aid to dependent children, and emergency assistance.

Significantly, the policy shift announced by the State Department on behalf of the administration made it clear that, despite repeated disclaimers throughout the eight-year asylum fight, the State Department—and not the Justice Department or the INS—had the primary responsibility for the denial of asylum to the Haitians.

As for the present, the Haitians are now under the additional protection of Judge King's landmark decision, staying the illegal procedures and acts against the 4,000 whose class-action suit had been before him. While the government is considering an appeal of Judge King's decision, the Haitians have a slender hold on due process. And the Carter administration's change of policy toward the Haitian "boat people," however belated, limited and incorrectly based, is an important breakthrough.

But the Haitians' struggle calls into question the commitment of the U.S. government to the achievement of human rights in this land and every land. It exposes the need for a foreign policy in and through which justice is discerned and practiced as the surest safeguard of security, peace and freedom in the Caribbean and anywhere else in the world. The struggle unmasks the specter of racial discrimination which haunts the refusal to treat the Haitians in the same way as Cubans, Vietnamese and others in flight from political repression and economic despair. Meanwhile, we can hope for the replacement of the Duvalier regime in Haiti by a government committed to end economic exploitation and political repression, and to a more just distribution of Haitian resources among Haitians themselves. Such a development would reduce considerably the numbers of Haitians now fleeing their homeland to the shores of Florida—a flight with perils so fierce and fateful that only political refugees would dare risk it.

ASIANS IN NEW YORK CITY[7]

On Main Street in Flushing, Queens, Korean vegetable stands and gift shops flourish alongside the delicatessens and drugstores, and the teen-agers who walk along the shopping thoroughfare punctuate their Chinese conversations with American slang.

In apartment buildings in the Bronx, Indochinese refugees gather in the lobbies, discussing the problems of making their way here and news of relatives from home.

In Woodside, Queens, a girl in designer jeans and spike-heeled sandals, her purple eye shadow striking as a neon light, escorts her elderly grandmother to the supermarket, the older woman in the drab pajamas of her native China.

[7] Excerpts from article entitled "Asian Refugees Strive for Safe Life in New World," by Anna Quindlen, staff reporter. New York *Times.* p B1+. Ag. 25, '80. © 1980 by The New York Times Company. Reprinted by permission.

And on Church Avenue in the Flatbush section of Brooklyn, the subway disgorges hundreds of tired riders in the evening who were once residents of Taiwan, Hong Kong, Saigon or Bangkok.

Number Placed at 400,000

They are New York's new Asians, and they have changed the way parts of the city look and feel. Two decades ago the majority of Asians here were Chinese, and were to be found below Houston Street in Manhattan. But, in the intervening years, their ranks have been augmented by Koreans, Vietnamese, Cambodians, Laotians, Thais, Filipinos and some Japanese.

There are also ever-growing numbers of new arrivals from China and nearly all of them, because of high rents in Manhattan and overcrowding in Chinatown, have moved into the neighborhoods where their counterparts from Europe settled more than a half century ago.

Many New Yorkers buy produce from the stands, flowers from the shops and food at the restaurants of the new East Asian immigrants. Also, the immigrants work in light factories and shoe factories, as seamstresses in the garment center and as accountants in midtown Manhattan. There are, by some estimates, more than 400,000 Asian Americans living in the city, many of them beset by problems of language and loneliness. But they are, with few exceptions, determined to make good here.

Most say they came to the United States for financial security and for the education of and a better future for their children. They say that they left home because of poverty or a repressive political regime. A revision of the immigration laws in 1965 made it possible for more to come to America; for some, the American withdrawal from Southeast Asia made the move imperative.

New York's East Asians have made parts of the city, some of them left vacant by the receding of earlier waves of immigrants, their own.

Change Since '64 Noted

"In 1964 when I came here to school, it was so hard to find a Korean store in New York," says Han Young Lee, who lives in Flushing with her husband, an accountant, and their 9-year-old daughter. "And there were just a few students here who all knew each other. Now there are grocery stores, vegetable stores, all the shops.

"Many old people move here because they can get whatever they want. And the new immigrants come because there is someone they can speak with in their language. And now people can find jobs in those places and that's another reason they come."

Flushing has indeed changed since Mrs. Lee came to America. . . . More than 20,000 of the city's 80,000 Koreans have settled in Flushing, most in the last decade. An additional 9,000 Koreans are coming to the city each year. And there are 70,000 Chinese living in Woodside, Elmhurst, Jackson Heights and other parts of Queens.

There are nearly 8,500 Asian students in the City University system; 1,000 of them are enrolled at City College, twice the number that attended a decade ago. In public schools in Queens alone, the number of Asian students attending has nearly tripled in 10 years.

The More Things Change

The Bronx and Brooklyn, too, reflect these new waves of immigrants and refugees for, since many of those coming from Indochina and from the rural areas of mainland China arrive without any knowledge of English and must take factory and restaurant jobs, they must be placed where rents are lowest.

On Church Avenue in Flatbush and on Davidson Avenue in the Bronx, there are some buildings that went begging until family after family of Asians was placed there by social welfare agencies or community groups.

"The idea that the Asians coming here are taking housing

and jobs away from the native-born is a myth," says Charles Wang, managing director of the Chinatown Planning Council, which has opened offices in Flushing and Flatbush in the last three years. "Landlords and employers say these are places they would have a hard time filling otherwise. Like lots of other people to come here from foreign countries, the immigrants will take these so they can save and buy a business or a house of their own."

In fact the attitudes and aspirations of the Asian immigrants and refugees mirror those of the immigrants who came before them. Land of opportunity, they say of America, place of freedom and money. Many say that they came here to re-unite their families. . . .

"If the Lamppole Had Feet . . ."

"Sometimes I can see that you do not know you are so lucky," says Cac Thanh Le, a urologist who is on welfare while studying for his qualifying exams in January. "We have a four-room apartment here, much better than the studio in Saigon. We are not free in Vietnam, in our action, in our thinking. We have a saying, 'If the lamppole had feet, it would not come here.'"

Maureen Sui, who immigrated five years ago, adds that people who wonder how immigrants and refugees tolerate tenement apartments and the overcrowding caused by several families living together are not familiar with conditions in Hong Kong. "Some people must rent bed space on eight-hour shifts," she says. "When your time is up, they wake you so the next person can have the bed."

Of course, the Asians who arrive here are faced with almost overwhelming problems as well. The primary one, the one all mention and the one most must fight to master, is the English language, which is so vastly different from their own. A range of organizations as well as the Board of Education offer English lessons for arriving immigrants and refugees, but until they have mastered the consonants they find so tongue-twisting many must take jobs far below their skills.

Engineer Swept Floors

Tang Kuei Te, an engineer for 13 years in Vietnam, recently got a job as a civil engineer with a construction company here, but before that he had a job sweeping in a supermarket in Brooklyn. He is working and saving for the eventual immigration of his wife and two children, whom he left in Taiwan. "I came here first to get the new life," he says slowly, searching for the words. "I don't know the U.S. life, but I know it is what we want. But first I must work hard, get money, get English."

Some Asians, however, have found ways to circumvent the new language. In Flushing, for example, there are now so many Koreans and Chinese and so many businesses owned by them—as many as 60 in the Main Street area, an association of Korean businessmen estimates—that their native tongue can be used both at and after work.

Many Koreans say one reason they want to own their own business is that it will lessen their problems with English. "No English, no English," say the two men running a small fruit stand near 41st Avenue on Main Street, their smiles wide. Some like it that way; others think that they must embrace their new home. Jungil Song, who opened a small variety shop off Main Street two years ago, says, "I am afraid of the future here."

"That it will turn into Koreatown?" asks Mrs. Lee.

"No, there are some bad people who are around here," he answers. "It would be better if there were more Koreans."

"Stabilizing Influence"

Some of their neighbors agreed. A Queens hairdresser whose window carries both Chinese and English characters says, "Some people are afraid this is going to turn into another Chinatown, but the people take such good care of their houses and their businesses that it is hard to argue with it."

"The Asians are generally perceived by their neighbors as

a stabilizing influence," says Frank Vardi, a population analyst in the Department of City Planning. "And we will probably never see the kind of ethnic concentration that we saw
earlier in this century. Chinese will live in Bay Ridge, but
they will have to compete with the Greeks for housing. You
see Flushing very visibly Asian, but there are many other ethnic groups as well. The days of the Chinatown are gone."

But the insecurities remain, many of them financial. Some
of the Indochinese refugees borrowed money to escape from
Vietnam and they work long hours or hold two jobs as they
struggle to repay their debts.

Dr. Le was determined not to take the public assistance
he and his family needed during the time he was studying for
his qualifying exams. "Then I was told of the income tax," he
says. "Now I know I will pay it back so I will take it. But I
prefer to use my own money."

"Financial security is very important," says Mr. Song,
"and the future for our children." The two are intertwined.

Many Asian parents say they have saved to buy a home in
Queens, where they feel that their family will be safer, have
more contact with other Asian children, and will be able to
attend bilingual classes in some of the schools. Some even pay
for their houses in cash because, as Mr. Wang says, "they
come in with their lifetime savings and do not want to spend
it on interest." They are concerned, they say, not that their
children will become Americanized, but that they will become simply bad people.

A Student's View

And their children sometimes think that their parents are
old-fashioned. "American parents, if their children want to do
things, they won't stop them," maintains George Hua, a 16-
year-old student at Bayside High School who has lived in
America for less than a year. "But Chinese parents always
want you to do the right thing."

Mrs. Lee adds: "Here is freedom. Parents are worried

about free dating and free choice of partner. We are trying to educate the children, before any decision they must consult their parents."

But as George and his friends, all in the current uniform of T-shirt, jeans and sneakers, make their way down Main Street they look like any other teen-agers, and Mrs. Lee and others admit that Asian parents will have some of the same problems that other immigrants had.

"All immigrants face the same experience, I suppose," says Chairman Kim, executive director of the Korean Community Services Center. "The first immigrants still observe the festivals, the costumes. The first generation will change very little. And when the second generation begins to change they will be unhappy. It happens everywhere."

SOVIET JEWS IN BRIGHTON BEACH[8]

In her native Russia, Ina Rodomskaya cherished a fairy tale vision of an America where all people were prosperous and free.

In four months here, her vision has changed in the reality of a one-bedroom basement apartment in a run-down . . . high-rise. She is still looking for a job. She is afraid of the elevators and long corridors in her building because of recent muggings and assaults. She is generally baffled by American ways.

And yet, as she tries to find her bearings, she is stubbornly optimistic about starting a new life at age 41. She has invested so much already—divorcing her husband after he did not want to emigrate, enduring the taunts of being a "traitor," losing her job as a college teacher. She did make the right decision to emigrate, she says, but with caution in her voice. If

[8] Excerpts from article entitled "A Myth for Soviet Jews," by Dusko Doder, staff writer. Washington *Post.* p A1+. Jl. 4, '80. © 1980 The Washington Post. Reprinted by permission.

nothing else, her 11-year-old son is assured of opportunities a Jew would never have in the Soviet Union.

The Human Drama

Rodomskaya's fate echoes many of the stories told by the 200,000 Soviet Jews who have emigrated in the last decade. It illustrates the human drama of the exodus from an authoritarian system as well as the difficulties faced by those who reach the West.

"We are like animals from a zoo suddenly freed," said journalist Yevgeny Rubin, 51, another recent arrival, trying to explain the trauma that the confrontation with freedom presents for Soviet citizens.

"Imagine you were born in prison and lived in it all your life, then [are] set free and you don't know what to do and where to go—you are in the jungle of freedom," Rubin said.

Most Soviet Jews "imagined America as a fairy tale story," explained Alex Zayats, 32, and this is largely a result of Soviet propaganda. The Soviet media, he said, "have been lying about so many things for such a long time that nobody believes anything the papers say. We, in fact, assumed that the opposite was true."

His father, a teacher in Odessa, didn't believe anything Soviet papers wrote about America and violence, Zayats said. "Exactly two weeks after we arrived here my father was robbed in downtown Manhattan."

Millions have emigrated from the Soviet Union in the past and have sacrificed greatly to come to the United States, but the new Soviet Jews are different.

They were released in an unprecedented move only after massive international pressure, and they were allowed to emigrate not to the United States but to Israel.

Israel is a painfully embarrassing issue to the immigrants. Israel sought them, and mounted a major effort to accommodate them. But 81,000 of the 200,000 given visas to leave the Soviet Union, have come to the United States instead.

Assistance Offered Immigrants

Most of those who have come here seem to have been
motivated by Horatio Alger mythology. There is irony in this,
because these immigrants have received social welfare assistance unknown to previous Russian immigrant groups. Elderly Soviet immigrants are eligible for Social Security, pensions, Medicare or Medicaid, welfare benefits and subsidized
housing. The younger ones are supported until they are
placed in jobs.

Two previous waves of Soviet immigrants—the first after
World War I and the second after World War II—received
no such assistance. The third wave has brought people who
are better educated, who are not interested in Jewish religious life and who are claiming from the start all the privileges and services available to them.

This has contributed to friction between the American
Jewish community and the "Russians." Critics say that resettlement efforts, like those provided by the New York Association for New Americans, called Nayana, merely reinforce the
Russian immigrants' inflated expectations and lead them to
demand more.

"All this assistance to ease their entry is also holding the
Russians from plunging into the American experiences as
other immigrants did," one Nayana official said privately.

On a different level, the Israeli government has been
pressuring American Jewish leaders to stop assistance to the
Russian immigrants and effectively force them to go to Israel.

Finally, cultural and psychological differences between
the latest Soviet immigrants and the established Jewish community here were obscured in the long political struggle to
pressure the Kremlin to "let our people go." These differences became pronounced in New York once the cause that
originally bound the two communities together no longer ex-
isted.

"The paradox is that in Russia I was a Jew and now I am a
Russian," say Yevgeny Ostrovsky, 41, a former interpreter

WYOMING VALLEY WEST HIGH SCHOOL

who immigrated here five years ago with his wife, who is also fluent in English.

Like other Moscow and Leningrad intellectuals, they emigrated for political reasons, mainly the question of individual liberties, he says. The sense of being Jewish, for the Ostrovskys, has no religious context, but is rather a reaction to what he calls "official anti-semitism" in the Soviet Union.

The Ostrovskys, . . . surrounded by all the accoutrements of middle class America, don't scorn "bourgeois" contentment. They have achieved it. And they proudly refer to their four-year-old daughter, who was born two months after they reached New York, as "a true American."

"It is like I have lived here all my life," said Mrs. Ostrovsky.

"My goal was to get out of Russia because I didn't like the system and I didn't like the country," says Ostrovsky, who now works as an editor for the *Novoye Ruskoye Slovo*, a Russian language newspaper with 50,000 daily circulation. "I didn't come to America to become rich, I came here to be free."

But most of his compatriots, Ostrovsky says, are leaving the Soviet Union for economic reasons. "They just come and they don't know why," he says, describing Jews from southern Russia and especially from the Black Sea port of Odessa as being "pushy, arrogant and greedy."

"The Odessa crowd" has settled at Brighton Beach, he said, not to create a new life but to recreate a little Russia.

Odessa on the Atlantic

Among Russian immigrants, Brighton Beach is known as the "Odessa on the Atlantic," the largest concentration of Soviet immigrants anywhere. Located on the southern tip of Brooklyn next to Coney Island, Brighton Beach is a red arc of massive apartment houses along a spectacular boardwalk, with smaller one- or two-family homes in back of the apartment houses.

More than a third of the community's 50,000 residents are
Soviet Jews who have settled here over the last five years.

Its restaurants bear Russian names. A "Black Sea" book-
store, a string of supermarkets, antique shops and other service establishments, all featuring Russian signs, testify to the
enormous entrepreneurial energy and talent of the immigrants.

The immigrants speak Russian and revert to past habits
easily. "Misha, that's one ruble eighty?" an elderly woman
asks a grocery clerk about the price of a bottle of wine, which
costs $1.80. "Yes, it's one ruble eighty," he responds in Rus-
sian.

There are other reminders of Russian life, such as bedding
and clothing hanging out the windows and a long line of
women and men, clutching pieces of paper, in front of Rabbi
Ezekiah Pikus' office at the Jewish Community Council store-
front office on the main street.

Providing Help

Sitting in 90-degree temperatures in a tiny cubicle of an
office, the rabbi is inundated by visitors and telephone callers,
seeking medical help, welfare, disability pensions, energy assistance supplements and job placement.

He explained to Yeva Krass, 41, that she and her husband
would be eligible for welfare once their Nayana checks are
stopped. The Krasses are receiving $150 a month each from
Nayana, plus a housing supplement.

Could the rabbi find a summer job for her 15-year-old son
Paul? Krass asked. The rabbi looked at the youth. "Would he
like to be a camp counselor in the mountains?" the rabbi
asked the mother. "No," the youth said looking at his mother.
"Why?" the rabbi shot back. "I don't know," the youth said
after a pause. "Is there something closer to home?" the
mother asked sheepishly. Both she and her husband suffer
from serious heart ailments.

In between phone calls, as he tries unsuccessfully to find
something for the youth in Brighton Beach, the rabbi explains

why this area was selected for resettlement. "It is similar to Odessa, the seashore and all, and the convenience of the shopping and transportation."

The rabbi deals with his tasks with a mixture of perplexity and frustration. So many practical problems before the council, he said, leave him no time to deal with spiritual questions. Besides, he said, the immigrants have been "alienated from any sort of religious feelings for over two generations now."

Now, said Joel Samuels, co-director of the Brighton Neighborhood Association, American Jews complain that some Russian Jews are using the yeshiva, or religious school, as a baby-sitting service and that their children disrupt classes.

Initial problems with the new immigrants were minor, Samuels said. "They would throw diapers out the window, or on the floors when washing them"—as they would do in Russia, where their floors were made of concrete. Various manuals in Russian were distributed to correct that, he said.

"Not Like the Old Immigrants"

But the real problem is that "they are not like the old immigrants—to them the U.S. citizenship doesn't mean much, they ignore invitations to community meetings or any meetings, they even wouldn't fill out census forms recently."

There are, however, many explanations for such behavior, said Alex Zayats, who works for Samuels as a liaison to the Russian community. "They are sick and tired of meetings they had to attend in the Soviet Union, of the voting that didn't mean anything, of filling out forms. They simply aren't prepared for this."

To the Russian immigrants, Rabbi Pikus and Samuels are persons of authority with whom they should establish personal contact.

They have grown up in a society in which public life is viewed as a fraud, regardless of who is in power, and in which men seek authority to get privileges and wealth, which they often do through corruption and stealing.

"America a Golden Land"

Soviet Jews, especially those from Odessa, are known as skillful manipulators whose knowledge of string-pulling is equaled only by Soviet Georgians. . . .

For the Brighton Beach police, the newcomers have brought few difficulties, although officers of the 60th Precinct have recently made an effort to learn Russian so they can deal with bar brawls as well as gang wars on the boardwalk between the Russians and Puerto Ricans.

But the main problem is car accidents, according to Detective Barry Brisacone. "The first thing when they come here is that they want to have a car, a big one, with or without a driver's license."

Brisacone and other non-Russians, however, are quick to say they believe that the influx of Russian Jews has not only "stabilized" the community, which a decade ago was on its way to becoming a slum, but has also revived its economic life.

In contrast to older and middle-aged immigrants, younger Soviet Jews have entered the mainstream of American life without difficulty. Some young businessmen already have made their first million.

In Brighton Beach, Mike Fidler, 55, and his wife, Ljuba, are busy making money in their restaurant, "Gasronom Moskva." He is "busy, busy, busy," said Fidler, and "I sleep well because I don't have to worry about what I can or cannot say."

Ljuba Fidler is so busy, she said, that she doesn't have a minute to fill out citizenship forms. "Too much paperwork," she said, serving piroshki (stuffed rolls) and vodka to customers.

And on the sidestreet, sitting outside her apartment building, Neha Doyben, 70, who came from Odessa with her three sons, was watching her grandchildren at play.

"America," she said, "is a golden land, a golden land."

THE LOS ANGELES MELTING POT[9]

A smog-dulled sun rises over a city that suddenly is the goal and dream of so many from so far away. The streets begin to fill as the stew of races and cultures that Los Angeles has become simmers and blends anew.

Vietnamese women squatting on Chinatown streets hawk fish. Old men in suspenders smoke their pipes in the shade of Armenian shops selling grape leaves, halvah and orange blossom water. On Hollywood Boulevard, a porno movie house is flanked by a Thai travel service and a Mongolian barbecue. Down the street, chiropractor Chin Lin's shingle tells passersby that Spanish is spoken within.

Though their numbers are impossible to estimate because so many are illegal aliens, more immigrants are coming to Los Angeles than to any other American city, federal and local officials say. Its relative proximity to Asia and Mexico makes it the natural "new wave" melting pot. And its movies and TV shows, exported world-wide and often depicting the town as a balmy, palm-lined paradise, have given it a familiarity and appeal that other places lack. Soviet emigre Zigmund Vays says simply: "I had a dream to live in a city full of sunshine."

So have many others. In 1960, the principal minority blocs here—blacks, Hispanics and Asiatics—together accounted for only 28% of the population. Rough estimates for 1980: 20% black, 30% Hispanic, 10% Asiatic and only 40% Anglo, out of a total population of 2.9 million. Much of the change has occurred within the past five years, which were marked by particularly heavy inflows of Mexicans, Vietnamese and Koreans.

The migrants add new tastes, new colors, new life to a ho-

[9] Reprint of article entitled "A Flood of Newcomers Is Turning Los Angeles into Tense Melting Pot," by Laurel Leff, staff reporter. *Wall Street Journal.* p 1+. S. 25, '80. Reprinted by permission of *The Wall Street Journal.* Copyright © 1980 Dow Jones & Company, Inc. All rights reserved.

mogenized sprawl of freeways, fast-food joints and ticky-tacky housing that critics have called "Double Dubuque." But the influx also brings strained city services, Tower of Babel schools in which teachers and pupils can't understand each other, apartments in which several people rotate sleeping hours in the same bed, and mounting racial-ethnic tensions.

Keeping the Lid On

"We're very concerned about the hostility here and the potential for a riot," says Carl Martin, executive director of the Los Angeles County Commission on Human Relations; he and everyone else here remember the carnage of the Watts riots in 1965. "We haven't had any overt, major incidents in recent years, and we're hoping the lid can be kept on," he adds.

But the pot is bubbling. There were 783 murders in the city last year, 50% more than in 1975. Many were due to gang warfare involving minorities battling for turf. For many immigrants, joining a gang gives them an identity and a measure of protection; in the sprawling barrio of East Los Angeles, three generations in the same house may belong to the same gang.

Blacks and Hispanics here have been fighting between and among themselves for many years, and so have rival Hong Kong and Taiwanese gangs, including the Wah Chings and Jo Fongs. Vietnamese of Chinese extraction now are joining them, and Korean gangs such as the American Burgers, Korean Killers and Black Ji are slugging it out with black and Hispanic gangs from adjoining neighborhoods.

There is mounting dissatisfaction with the Los Angeles police department, which is still 81% white, over its treatment of racial and ethnic minorities. The black community has been sharply critical of what it considers unwarranted police shootings, and some Vietnamese have complained to social-service agencies that officers have called them "gooks" and "mama-sans."

The department is stepping up minority hiring and is training officers in dealing with minorities. It has also set up special units such as the Asian task force, formed six years ago to battle crime in burgeoning Asian neighborhoods.

But the police, like practically every agency in town, have run afoul of the language problem. "If someone calls who doesn't know English, there's an 85% chance the person he's talking to won't even know what language he's speaking," says Ron Wakabayashi, who runs a drug-rehabilitation center here. A task force officer complains that operators shuttle a person speaking any tongue that they can't identify, including Arabic, to his unit. Even if an Asian gets through, there may be head-scratching; though all of Asian extraction themselves, only about half the task-force officers speak a foreign language—and the caller may be Thai, Vietnamese, Filipino, Japanese, Chinese, Korean or something else.

Currently, 83 languages are spoken in Los Angeles County, and every agency in the area is beating the bushes for bilingual employes. The schools, however, are most affected by the profusion of tongues.

Hollywood High, where 60 languages and dialects are spoken in students' homes, has "a real communication problem," Homer Gansz, the principal, says. At a recent parents' night, all the speeches had to be translated from English into Korean, Armenian and Spanish. "It took 25 minutes to get through one three-minute spiel. What a fiasco!" Mr. Gansz says.

The state requires that a school form a bilingual class when 20 or more students in any grade speak a specific foreign tongue as their first language. Now dozens of schools in the mammoth Los Angeles district have two, three or four qualifying minorities in everything from Tongan to Farsi; in all, the district needs 2,000 more bilingual teachers and can't find them all. So, in many classrooms, the frustrated simply go on trying to teach the baffled.

The extent of the alien influx and the transience of many immigrants turn confusion into chaos; schools are packed with students whose ethnic mix keeps shifting. In Hollywood, a prime entry point, 95% of the new pupils enrolled at Grant Elementary School in the past few months speak no English. Currently, the school is scrambling for teachers who speak Spanish, Korean, Armenian and Tagalog. But the list could change quickly. The average length of enrollment there is only 10 weeks; the shortest was four hours.

The Hoover Street School, which had only 452 students 15 years ago, now has almost 2,000 and expects nearly 3,000 by 1984. While classrooms are gradually emptying in the city's biggest Anglo enclave, the San Fernando Valley, those in parts of the city where immigrants settle are getting as jam-packed as Hoover.

In July, the district put 50 schools with 75,000 students into year-round operation to ease the pressure. But Byron Kimball, district deputy director for planning, says at least 10 new schools costing a total of more than $120 million still should be built. "The district can't raise that money on its own," he frets.

Medical Problems

Health-care costs are going through the roof, too, and the county is suing the federal government to recover $89 million that it spent on treating illegal aliens alone in 1976–78. It plans to add last year's costs, a huge $109 million, to the tab.

Many immigrants bring unwelcome company to the states—tuberculosis, leprosy and typhoid. "We now have one of the highest urban TB rates," says Dr. Shirley Fannin, chief of acute communicable disease control for the Health Services Department. Rates in Chicago and New York are declining, but the incidence in Los Angeles continues to climb, Dr. Fannin says. She notes that the Vietnamese are particularly susceptible. Treating TB alone this year will cost $4.2 million, and she says she is "floundering around" seeking funds.

"Hotbedding"—jamming two, three and even four families into one apartment where they often sleep in shifts—is aggravating health problems and adding to school crowding.

There is little else many immigrants can do. Los Angeles has the country's lowest rental vacancy rate—under 1% compared with 6% nationally. The few spaces available cost far more than most immigrants can afford.

So the landlord, of course, must be deceived. One Vietnamese man recently put up 13 homeless countrymen in his one-bedroom apartment; at 6 a.m. he packed them into a van and dumped the bewildered horde at the beach. He sneaked them back in at 9 p.m. "They slept all in a row from the bedroom through the kitchen; no one could move. It was crazy," he recalls.

Ethnic Enclaves

As they do elsewhere, alien newcomers to the City of the Angels cluster in ethnic enclaves where English is the foreign tongue, where culture shock is cushioned by sights and smells reminiscent of home. Such enclaves range from a single apartment house filled with immigrants from Riga, Latvia, to cities within the city such as East Los Angeles, the barrio that is home to more people of Mexican extraction than any other place outside Mexico City itself.

More pockets of aliens are becoming full-blown neighborhoods. In 1970, only about 10,000 Koreans were here; now there are more than 100,000, most living in or near a district called "Koreatown," with its own restaurants, shops and businesses. It has a Korean fishing club, a Korean temperance union, and 111 churches to repent in.

As they realize a piece of the American dream, some immigrants imitate American city dwellers and move to outlying suburban towns. Armenians favor Glendale, Chinese move to Monterey Park, and Japanese like Gardena.

And for entrepreneurial newcomers with a little cash, Los Angeles offers opportunities to earn their way out to the suburbs. Business brokers here say more than half their clientele now are foreign-born; Koreans, who tend to be better-educated and more affluent than most other groups, are believed to run about 6,000 businesses here.

Even the fortunate, however, discover on arrival that the city isn't as Hollywood has painted it and that it can be harsh, even terrifying. "Koreans see movies and think all Americans are beautiful people living in mansions," says the Rev. Matthew Ahn, who heads a community-service group here. "But when they get here, they find it isn't a safe city. They see helicopters with search-lights overhead, they see wounded people on the TV news, and they're scared to death."

Ironically, immigrants also have trouble adjusting to the other immigrants and minorities they find here. Many Asians have ingrained prejudices against, and fear of, blacks. They don't necessarily get along with other Asians, either; though Anglos lump them together as one minority, the Asians include dozens of nationalities and regional groups with a history of animosity in their home countries. "We've been fighting each other for centuries," one Japanese-American says.

Restless Blacks

Unskilled immigrants from traditional rural societies have the hardest adjustment of all. Jo Marcel, head of the county's Indochina social-service project, says wife-beating, divorce and alcoholism are all rising as the Indochinese struggle with a foreign urban culture, ideas such as women's liberation and even indoor plumbing. "Some of these people don't even know how to use a toilet," he says.

Most newcomers must settle for rock-bottom jobs. Some become the pawns of employers who play off one minority against another to keep wages low. Recently more than a dozen Vietnamese hired by an assembly plant in the San Fernando Valley complained of harassment from Hispanic co-workers; the community agency that got them the positions discovered that the Vietnamese had replaced Hispanics fired because they had wanted to start a union.

The influx of foreigners also is creating restlessness in Watts and other predominantly black areas of south-central Los Angeles, where youth unemployment hovers at about 50%. "We are opening our arms to immigrants, but we aren't opening our arms to our own black citizens who've been here much longer," says John Mack, president of the Los Angeles Urban League. Adds an AFL-CIO official here: "Charity should begin at home."

Blacks, however, have political influence the others lack. Mayor Tom Bradley is black, and so are three of the 15 city councilmen—while Hispanics, by far the biggest minority and possibly a majority within 10 or 20 years, haven't any elected representatives in city government. That may change. One political analyst says: "As the Anglos fade, you may see the blacks running the political establishment and the Chicanos fighting them for power."

Meanwhile, more people keep coming. Some 200 miles south, they penetrate the border, move north by night and melt into "East Los," uncounted and uncountable. They come from Russia, Samoa, Manila. Some 1,500 Indochinese are arriving every month, mostly after stays in other American cities; they like the climate in Los Angeles and are drawn by the presence of so many countrymen. Smiling in the sunlight, one recent arrival says cheerfully: "After a year or two, we all move here."

III. AMERICANIZATION: QUESTIONS OF LANGUAGE AND CULTURE

EDITOR'S INTRODUCTION

All immigrants, whether voluntary travelers or fleeing refugees, face the task of beginning a new life in a new land. The land may offer sanctuary and welcome or hostility and resentment, but whatever their reception the newcomers must meet the challenge of adapting themselves and making a fresh start. For many the barriers are formidable. Economically, if they are not to remain public charges, they must quickly find a way to earn a livelihood. Culturally, too, they must adapt, especially if they are young, have young children, and are determined to become part of the mainstream. How immigrants, and the American community as a whole, can cope with the hurdles of assimilation is the concern of the excerpts in this section.

The first article focuses on those who have chosen to make a permanent commitment to their adopted country; the "landmark day" on which the naturalized American takes the citizen's Oath of Allegiance is described by Philip W. Shenon of the *Wall Street Journal*.

Retaining the old tongue while learning the new is one of the means by which some groups seek to make the transition. But bilingualism—more precisely, bilingual education—has fired its own controversies. These battles are covered in a selection from *Time;* a *Wall Street Journal* story by Gerald F. Seib; and an article opposing bilingual programs by teachers' union president Albert Shanker, printed in the New York *Times.*

Relationships between the growing Chicano minority and the Anglo mainstream of society are analyzed in an excerpt from the book *The Golden Door,* by Professor Paul R. Ehrlich, Professor Loy Bilderback, and Anne H. Ehrlich. The concluding article is a New York *Times* report on the Hispanic press and the development of United States-style journalism, by Rudy Garcia, former executive editor of *El Diario-La Prensa*, a New York Spanish-language daily.

THE OATH OF ALLEGIANCE[1]

Wiera Zvicevicius is up before seven on her landmark day. She breakfasts hurriedly on a piece of toast daubed with marmalade, and bathes. Then she puts on the frilly, rose-red dress made just for this occasion.

By 9:00 A.M. the sun has broken through the clouds over Boston harbor. Mrs. Zvicevicius, her cheeks a color to match her dress, is already waiting expectantly in line outside venerable Faneuil Hall. "Today is big day," she says, struggling with a language that 50 years in Poland have made impossible to master. "Today become American."

In three hours the cleaning lady with the long name will join 484 others in an oath renouncing "fidelity to any foreign prince, potentate, state or sovereignty." With those words they will gain what has been yearned for by generations of foreign-born people sapped by poverty, crushed by the state, or trapped under the muttering guns of war—the privileges and responsibilities of U.S. citizenship.

America may not be the golden place it once was or seemed to be. Its cities may be decaying, its opportunities crimped by recession, its global power trimmed. But for the people in line here, it is still the land of hope. "This is good country," declares Mrs. Zvicevicius. "No Russian here. Here is freedom—and much, much food." And she laughs.

Others apparently agree. The U.S. puts no limit on the

[1] Reprint of article entitled "For Immigrants, Oath of Allegiance Caps a Long Journey," by Philip W. Shenon, staff reporter. *Wall Street Journal.* p 1+. O. 17, '80. Reprinted by permission of *The Wall Street Journal.* Copyright © 1980 Dow Jones & Company, Inc. All rights reserved.

number of immigrants who can become citizens, and this year about 190,000 are expected to do so, almost double the number 10 years ago. In Boston alone, 5,000 men and women will be naturalized in 1980.

Of History and Ghosts

The recent ceremony, officially called the final U.S. District Court hearing on naturalization, is a joyful, noisy affair held in the dignified old brick hall. It is a place encrusted with history and full of ghosts.

In 1775, a motley gang of Massachusetts rebels met here to plot strategy against the army of a detested king; today hundreds of kids, the children of immigrants, swing on 200-year-old banisters and shout along plastered halls where Samuel Adams and Paul Revere once walked.

The kids are important. Often fluent in two languages, they are the translators and paper-work expediters for their parents, who are shuffling forward in a series of lines as the federal immigration bureaucracy takes one last swipe at them. A Mr. Yee, for example, has apparently written on a form that he was married for the first time within the past year. His seven-year-old son, a seeming contradiction to that statement, glibly explains to a puzzled clerk that his father has made a mistake. It is corrected, and the Yees move on.

Some citizenship applicants here speak good English and know more about the U.S. than do many native-born citizens. But many others won't fully understand the purpose of the ceremony, the words of the judge who presides, or the history of the Stars and Stripes whipping in the breeze outside.

It is, in fact, easy to become a citizen. An applicant must have lived in the U.S. at least five years, must not have been a Communist Party member within the last 10, and must not have been in jail more than 180 days. He is required to have a grasp only of "simple" English, a standard that is very loosely interpreted.

Finally, he is expected to know basic U.S. history and civics. Although about 10% of applicants are rejected for one reason or another, it's said that virtually no one flunks the history and civics quiz. It's just too simple.

An Innocent Patriotism

Carlos Manuel Gil, a 29-year-old fisherman who comes from Portugal, admits to a profound ignorance of American history. He passed the oral quiz, he says, by blurting out one of the few names he knew in answer to a question he didn't. "I just say George Washington was the first," he recalls. "I guess right."

But if the applicants stumble over their English and if they don't know who Paul Revere was, they do have a qualification evidently more important to Uncle Sam: They want very much to be Americans. There is about the people in the old hall an innocent, almost childlike patriotism that never fails to move even those who have witnessed this scene many times.

One such observer is George McGrath, the ruddy-faced clerk of the court and veteran of nearly 100 naturalization ceremonies. "These people restore your faith," he says. "They really love this country. They appreciate America." In 1978, he recalls, the century's worst blizzard shut down Boston, and with it the scheduled naturalization proceedings. Some immigrants, dressed in their Sunday best, somehow struggled here through the drifts, anyway. Rather than disappoint them, an impromptu ceremony was held.

As applicants shuffle along the corridors, they collect a selection of patriotic songs and sayings, words for the Oath of Allegiance, and a boilerplate letter from President Carter beseeching them to help make America "a more wonderful place in which to live." An Australian woman carefully folds the letter and keeps it. "How nice of Mr. Carter to write us," she says.

Two women wearing blue military-style caps stick American flag pins in the lapels of applicants going by. They are Evelyn Curtin and Bessie Mentis, co-chairwomen of the Americanism committee of the local American Legion women's auxiliary. Mrs. Curtin, a matronly, white-haired woman who has been doing "flag duty" for 10 years, says: "Some of these people are so happy they run and kiss you." Mrs. Mentis adds that "it's real gratifying" and only hopes that all of them *really* want to be citizens.

If Mrs. Mentis needs reassurance, she should meet Thomas Tom, now 30. One night eight years ago, he left his father's rice paddies in mainland China, made his way to the coast, and swam five inky miles of the South China Sea. Dodging gunboats, Mr. Tom reached Hong Kong six hours later. A slight, quiet man who speaks better English than some immigrants who have been here 20 years, he now is a waiter in a Chinese restaurant in Attleboro.

Mr. Tom has no rosy illusions about America. Boston toughs have yelled racial slurs at him in the streets, and he sees streaks of selfishness and materialism in the American character. "Americans are sometimes bad," he says sadly. "They take advantage of freedom because they have too much." But he adds: "This is a turning point for me. China had no freedom."

It is now a few minutes before noon. Behind a big pine door, Robert E. Keeton, justice of the U.S. District Court for Massachusetts, is pulling on his heavy black robe. Like his colleagues, he considers his duty today "one of the great pleasures of the job"—in part, he adds, because it's the only time his verdict pleases everybody. Ready now, he sweeps into the packed hall, trailed by his entourage of clerks and immigration officials.

The ceremony lasts 25 minutes, and its climax is the Oath of Allegiance. The children quiet down, the people rise and raise their right hands. Some voices break as the new citizens vow to defend a Constitution some of them still don't understand against "all enemies, foreign and domestic."

Mrs. Zvicevicius, standing out like a beacon in her pretty red dress, is dabbing at her eyes. Mr. Gil, the fisherman who confesses he still gets the Civil War and the Revolutionary War mixed up, strains intently to see the podium.

In a minute it is over, and a cheer goes up in the hall. The crowd bursts through the doors to the outside, where there are more tears, hugs and picnics on the green. Mr. Tom can't celebrate, however. He worked late last night, had to get up early to be here, and is going straight home. "Must sleep," he says. "Have to start new life wide-awake."

BATTLE OVER BILINGUALISM[2]

"Let's go," the little boy urges, tugging impatiently at his mother's blouse. *"Un momento,"* she replies, searching the bustling hallway for the bright red T shirt of her other son. *"¿Dónde está Miguel?"* A moment later, Miguel bursts through the throng of chattering children and appears at his mother's side. *"¿Qué vamos supper, Mom?"* he asks. *"What's for supper?"*

For Miguel, 8, a student at the 91% Mexican American Briscoe Elementary School on Houston's sweltering east side, such easy leaps from language to language are an everyday matter. In his bilingual third-grade class, Miguel takes science, math and language arts in both English and Spanish, his native tongue. Typically, a one-hour science lesson is taught one day in English. The next day the teacher covers the same material, but in Spanish. Ideally, after two or three years of this bilingual barrage, Miguel will master enough English to do all his classwork in that language.

If the program worked just that way, there would be no problem. But Miguel's curriculum is a tiny part of a crazy quilt of local, state and national attempts to cope with the growing number of U.S. schoolchildren, some 3.5 million of them, for whom English is a second language. Now lumped under the heading of bilingual education, these efforts began with special ESL (English as a second language) classes. Later came attempts to teach children in their native tongue for a few years so they would not fall behind while they learned

[2] Reprint of article from *Time.* 116:64–5. S. 8, '80. Reprinted by permission from TIME, The Weekly Newsmagazine; Copyright Time Inc. 1980.

English. In 1968 Congress passed the Bilingual Education Act giving non-English-speaking children the option to study in their native tongue as a means of easing their way into U.S. life. To educators, that process is known as "transition." But over the years, with the help of the Federal Government, the Supreme Court and demands for aid from large Hispanic groups, the program expanded to include biculturalism. And more and more it seems to be headed toward what educators call "maintenance," which means encouraging children to stay in special native-language courses for years.

Supporters see bilingual ed as a vast improvement over the sink-or-swim school techniques that Americanized earlier immigrants. Says Awilda Orta, director of New York City's office of bilingual education: "People who feel good about their past heritage will be more productive citizens." But critics regard bilingual education as expensive, inefficient and above all un-American. Says Diane Ravitch of Columbia University's Teachers College: "There are cases of third-generation Puerto Ricans in bilingual classes. That just doesn't make sense."

In 1969 the whole program affected 25,000 children. This year the federal program alone will handle an estimated 500,-000. Begun as a local option available to poor children who are weak in English, bilingual ed is now a federally enforceable right for children speaking any one of 70 native tongues, from Yupik to Yapese, from Vietnamese to Russian. Collectively it costs Americans $700 million a year. It will soon cost more. With schools reopening next week, the Department of Education will launch public hearings in six cities (Chicago, Denver, New York, New Orleans, San Antonio and San Francisco) about Government proposals for regulating and reinforcing the program.

Where the Program Is Concentrated

The difficulty of evaluating or enforcing rules for bilingual education is evident from even a brief look at the areas where much of the money and effort for the program are concentrated:

☐ Chicago now has about 500,000 Spanish-speaking citizens—Mexicans, Puerto Ricans and Cubans—totaling well over 10% of the population. One-third of the Hispanic students need some kind of bilingual education, and the cost of providing it has soared by more than 800% in the past eight years. Illinois law requires that when 20 or more English-deficient students of the same language background are enrolled in the same class, a bilingual program must be provided. Because the Spanish programs have been taught longer, Hispanics do reasonably well. Programs for newer ethnic groups—among them some 10,000 Japanese, 10,000 Chinese and 10,000 Filipinos—have been less effective. Last June an amendment calling for a total cutoff of bilingual funding passed the Illinois house but was rejected by the state senate.

☐ In Texas, where Mexican children used to be shamed, spanked—and sometimes expelled— for speaking Spanish in school, 160,000 youngsters like Miguel are being taught in Spanish. To counteract "the Alamo mentality" and reinforce long bruised ethnic pride, the children sing Mexican songs and do Mexican dances. "Children need to know that not everyone came over on the Mayflower," says State Senator Carlos Truan. Bilingual ed students also take tests every year in English skills to see if they can be "exited" into mainstream classes. Critics point out that unlike earlier waves of U.S. immigrants from Europe, Mexican Americans in Texas move back and forth over the border to their former homeland and so are unlikely to be fully assimilated. As to learning English, Bilingual Teacher Faye Brown of Houston notes that children learn fastest when driven by need and desire. They learn in sports, for instance, when instructions and rules are given only in English. Television also serves to spur the children. Says another teacher: "They're just dying to understand what's going on in *The Incredible Hulk.*"

☐ The city of Los Angeles has more than 2 million Spanish-speaking residents. But Mexican Americans are spread all over the state, placing a bilingual burden on small school systems too. Of California's 3.9 million schoolchildren, nearly 10% so far have been defined as limited, or non-English-speaking. The bilingual program suffers from a lack of adequate teachers. Says State Board of Education President Michael Kirst: "We need 9,000 teachers. We only have 5,000, and the demand is growing faster than the supply."

□ In Dade County, Fla., Spanish was legally considered a second language even before the latest wave of Cuban refugees. There are 54,000 Spanish-speaking students now in Dade County's bilingual programs. But, says Lavona Zuckerman, a member of the citizens advisory committee, "in Miami we have leaned over backward for 20 years to accommodate the refugees. Learning in Spanish has made children feel comfortable in Spanish. Our compassion is making us a nation of ethnic minorities first, rather than Americans first." Proponents of the program insist, however, that bilingual children are doing nearly as well academically as English-speaking children.

□ New York City, by tradition the largest and most famous immigrant gateway to the New World, now has 80,000 children in bilingual classes. About 60,000 are Spanish. Among the nine other languages: Arabic, Chinese, Greek, Haitian Creole, Hebrew, Korean and Russian. Naturally, in the shadow of Ellis Island, there are many nostalgic references to the melting pot and the role of the American high school in giving incoming foreigners their first shared experience of the American way of life. Proponents argue that what was best for grandfather is not good enough for immigrant children today. For one thing, grandfather often never really learned English in the melting-pot school. For another, he could get a job right out of elementary school. The local political struggle over bilingual schools is fiercest in New York too. A black critic recently described the program as "a Puerto Rican employment program."

Bilingual Education: How Effective?

One reason discussion of bilingual education generates more partisan heat than pragmatic light is that its academic effectiveness is hard to measure. Shockingly, very little hard effort thus far has even been made to measure it. Critics and proponents alike have few real facts to go on. Both seem to agree that in the hands of a good teacher, bilingual programs reduce the high dropout rate among non-English-speaking students. They also agree that there is a terrible shortage of good bilingual teachers.

Secretary of Education Shirley Hufstedler admits the program needs improvement. The Federal Government's aim, under law, she notes, has always been transition. Where maintenance occurs, it is the result of local or state initiatives. One of the subjects at next week's public hearings is just what sort of federal limit should be set on the number of years a child can stay in the program.

The only national study of bilingual ed was completed in 1977 by the California-based American Institutes for Research. After studying 11,500 students over two years, researchers found that children in bilingual programs did no better at learning English or anything else than non-English-speaking students thrust into regular classes—except for a slight edge in elementary math. Proponents of bilingualism, including Hufstedler, regard the report not only as inadequate but out of date. Says Rudolph Troike, director of the office of multicultural bilingual education at the University of Illinois: "The payoff of bilingual education doesn't show up until the fifth or sixth year of instruction." Most critics wonder if the educational system and the taxpayers can wait that long for an answer.

ENGLISH AND THE MELTING POT[3]

Tien So Do, an 11-year-old Vietnamese refugee, presents a perplexing educational problem. She is bright-eyed, healthy and eager to learn—and she knows practically no English.

School officials here in Fairfax County [Virginia] believe they know how to help her. Tien is learning English in an intensive class that occupies most of her school day. As she begins mastering English, she will move into some regular classes, and within two years she should be learning all subjects with her peers.

Fairfax County is proud of this program. But minority organizations and federal education officials believe Tien is being cheated. They contend that schools should have to offer students like her bilingual education—that is, teach them such basic subjects as mathematics and social studies in their native language while they learn English.

The idea seems noble enough. Bilingual education is designed to prevent foreign-language students from falling behind in other academic areas while they are busy learning English. "How can you really argue that using a child's home language won't help him?" wonders Tracy Gray, an official in the U.S. Department of Education's Bilingual Education Office.

But bilingual education is stirring up an emotional national debate—"so much so, in fact, that the future of this promising pedagogical tool is uncertain," writes Alan Pifer, president of Carnegie Corp., in the organizations's . . . [1979] annual report.

Although some schools already have bilingual education, opponents argue it is at best unproven and at worst a confusing teaching method that will prevent children from ever learning English properly. Some even fear that offering bilin-

[3] Reprint of article by Gerald F. Seib, member of Washington bureau. *Wall Street Journal.* p 28. 0. 9, '80. Reprinted by permission of *The Wall Street Journal.* © 1980 Dow Jones & Company, Inc. All rights reserved.

gual education to the waves of immigrant children descending on U.S. schools could create a fractured, multilingual nation lacking the bond of a common language.

"To the extent that we recognize bilingualism, 50 or 60 years down the road we will have a different set of problems," warns Albert Shanker, president of the American Federation of Teachers.

Above all, though, some critics think the Education Department has overstepped the federal government's bounds by proposing regulations that would force local school systems to offer bilingual education. Already, congressional foes are trying to kill the bilingual regulations, which the department hopes to put into effect by the end of this year.

The regulations are an outgrowth of a 1974 Supreme Court ruling, *Lau v. Nichols*, in which the court held that schools that don't provide special help to foreign-language students violate their civil rights. The ruling overturned a federal appeals court decision that it wasn't discriminatory for San Francisco to refuse to teach English to Chinese-speaking students, a decision issued over the strong dissent of Appeals Court Judge Shirley Hufstedler, now the U.S. Secretary of Education.

The Supreme Court didn't specifically require bilingual programs, though. And even proponents of bilingual education concede that educators have done little research on whether it will work.

Nevertheless, the Education Department believes that to fully comply with the intent of the *Lau* ruling, schools should offer bilingual programs. Ideally, a teacher fluent in both English and a foreign language would teach basic subjects in the foreign language. Students would also spend time studying English.

The Fairfax County Case

For school districts like the one here in Fairfax, an affluent county just outside Washington, adopting bilingual programs would mean big headaches. Fairfax County sprawls over 405 square miles and, with 163 schools and 128,000 students, has the nation's 10th largest school system.

In many ways, the system is the melting pot come to life. About 6,000 of its students are foreign-born, and about 2,700 need special language instruction. Its foreign-tongued students, most of them recent immigrants, speak more than 50 different languages.

About half the foreign-language students speak one of three tongues—Spanish, Vietnamese and Korean—but languages such as Urdu, Farsi and Swahili are also represented. Often, only a handful of students speak a given language. And at some schools, as many as 15 foreign languages are spoken by students.

Providing bilingual programs for such a diverse group would be chaotic if not impossible, argues Esther Eisenhower, director of the system's intensive-English program. Competent teachers and teaching materials simply aren't available in many languages. "Where in the world might I find a certified teacher in Urdu or Farsi?" she asks.

The proposed regulations seek to deal with some of these problems. For example, if a school has only a few students speaking a given language, the school could satisfy the requirements by using roving teachers, parent-of-student tutors or tape recordings.

But Mrs. Eisenhower contends that such methods would dilute the quality of education for foreign-language students. "Isn't it ironic that we are relegating these people to be taught by less-than-qualified teachers just because they speak Urdu or Swahili?" she asks.

Meanwhile, county officials contend they have proved that their intensive English-as-second-language, or ESL, program works. By teaching students English as quickly as possible, they say, the program prepared students not only for school life but for survival in an English-speaking society.

And the officals assert that students don't fall behind in other subjects. From the outset, foreign-language students take physical education and music with their English-speaking peers. Early in their ESL training, they move into regular classes in such subjects as mathematics and science, which don't require extensive language skills.

As proof of ESL's effectiveness, the district proudly claims that fourth and sixth graders leaving the ESL program in 1977 scored over the 40th percentile on a national test of general educational level. Two years later, they scored over the 50th percentile.

Under the proposed regulations, a school system like Fairfax County's might obtain a waiver from some of the bilingual requirements if it can demonstrate to the government that its program is working. But the idea of asking for a waiver rankles Mrs. Eisenhower.

"Waiver implies illegality, that you are on the wrong side of the law but some benevolent judge has decided to let you go," she says. In short, she finds the idea of the federal government dabbling in the county's programs "heresy."

Minorities Are Rallying

But minority groups are rallying behind the government's bilingual proposal. They argue that schools, with some exceptions, have ignored the problems of foreign-speaking students, often merely immersing them in English-only classes. The result has been poor performance and high dropout rates.

Now, proponents say, the government needs to step in and guarantee children the simple right to learn in a language they understand. "Absent the regulations, it's another generation of kids down the drain," says Tomas Saucedo, an education researcher at the National Council of La Raza, a Hispanic advocacy group.

Advocates don't view the issue as a choice between bilingual education and intensive-English programs. They insist that good intensive-English instruction must be part of any complete bilingual program. Indeed, bilingual proponents say parents' generally strong desire that their children learn fluent English should deflate any fears that bilingual education will create a fractured society without a dominant language.

"You talk to any Hispanic parents and they're going to tell you they want their kid to learn English," says Ms. Gray of the Education Department. "That's not even an issue now."

But at the same time parents don't want their children embarrassed because they haven't yet learned English. Nor do they want their children's skills in their native language stamped out in English-only schools.

Purging a child of his mother tongue cuts his ties to his cultural heritage, breaks down communication with his parents and generally reinforces "the myth of Anglo supremacy," says Michael Olivas, director of research at Lulac National Education Service Centers, a Hispanic organization.

Advocates say that one of the advantages of bilingual education is that students emerge with both proficiency in English and improved skills in their native language. Thus, bilingual advocates find it particularly ironic that bilingual education has stirred such a fuss at the time educators generally agree that schools need to encourage more U.S. students to learn foreign languages.

Minority organizations realize that beating back the opponents of bilingual education may be a tough job. But they consider it one of their top priorities in the 1980s. "I do frame this as a civil rights issue, no more so or less so than desegregation or any other civil rights issue," says Mr. Olivas.

THE CASE AGAINST BILINGUALISM[4]

The new Department of Education has issued a set of proposed regulations on the education of children whose original language was not English. The proposal is an unmitigated disaster. It threatens the fabric of American education and

[4] Reprint of "Where We Stand: Can U.S. Force Schools to Go Bilingual?" column appearing as advertisement in New York *Times,* by Albert Shanker, president, United Federation of Teachers. New York *Times.* p E7. Ag. 24, '80. © 1980 by Albert Shanker. Reprinted by permission.

the future of our country. The public should bring pressure on President Carter and Secretary of Education Shirley Hufstedler so that the plan is abandoned.

Back in 1974 the Supreme Court decided in *Lau v. Nichols* that it was not enough for a school district to provide the same education for a child who could not understand English as it provided for children who do. The decision deserved support. Obviously, when a child who speaks and reads no English is put into a regular class, the child cannot be expected to understand or to learn.

The Court did not say what should be done. It just ordered that something be done, something which recognized the special needs and problems of the non-English-speaking child. The Court suggested some approaches: "Teaching English to students of Chinese ancestry who do not speak the language is one choice. Giving instruction in Chinese is another. There may be others."

While the Court demanded that something special be done, it left open the question of the specific program to be used. It was to be left to educators to decide on just what is the best educational method . . . and to local school boards, elected by the people in their communities to oversee the schools. It was appropriate for the federal government to state and define the law, right for qualified professional educators to find the best educational methods and within the political province of local school boards to adapt programs to local conditions and needs.

Furthermore, there is no evidence that any given method of teaching children who do not speak English is better than another. Were there overwhelming evidence that one approach was successful while others were not, it might make sense to mandate the successful program. Where no such evidence exists, it makes sense to allow for professional and local choice . . . and for widespread experimentation so that better programs can be developed.

Now, despite the lack of evidence that one program is better than another, the Administration proposes to mandate one program for the majority of other-language children, whether or not that is the choice of the teacher, the principal, or the local school district. That program is bilingual education, instruction in the child's original language while the child is learning English.

Under the new rules, children from other countries with a different native language will be instructed in English if their English is superior to their use of their native language. Such children are few in number. Those who are superior in their native language—almost all—and whose English ability is at a level with 40% of *all* the students in the same grade nationally or statewide must be taught in both languages. In other words, unless an immigrant child is nearly at or above the average for native-born children, the child must be taught in both languages.

School districts will have to comply or face federal prosecution. They will need thousands of bilingual teachers—who are not available. They will be required to retrain their existing staff to become bilingual—a noble goal but one which is difficult and expensive and adds to the great burdens already faced by a classroom teacher. But also, while the existing teachers are learning to speak a second language, the regulations require that, "... other bilingual individuals ... provide services in the interim." In other words, instruction will be given by individuals not licensed or certified to teach. The Administration has determined—without any empirical evidence—that children from Spanish, Chinese, Italian, Vietnamese and many other backgrounds will learn more if taught in both languages by someone other than a teacher than if they are taught intensively to learn English by a regular teacher.

Still another section of the regulations sounds good but, in light of the previous conflicts on this issue, it may have ominous consequences. The regulations require educational programs and activities to be "operated with respect for the culture and cultural heritage of the ... limited-English-proficient students." Does this mean just what it says? If so, there can be no argument. But it may mean much more. If a Puerto Rican teacher is employed to teach Mexican American children, could this be viewed as a lack of respect for the Mexican culture and heritage? Will this section be used to enforce the notion that only teachers of the same ethnic origins can teach their own?

The issues raised by the proposed federal regulations are huge. Should the U.S. government impose particular educational programs? Can it mandate programs which are still experimental and whose superiority has not been demonstrated? Can it override professional judgment and local control? And, should it impose huge new costs on hard-pressed local school districts? The government estimates the cost at between $180 million and $591 million, but that is like its estimate of the cost of educating the handicapped and of other programs. It will be much, much more, and with money in short supply, it will be taken from other current educational programs. Money that could be used to teach English intensively to these very children will be used for testing, placement and teacher language training.

But the biggest issue of all is the question of bilingualism. Will federal programs lead the U.S. to become another Quebec? The American people come from many cultures, many language backgrounds. One of the major purposes of the American public school has been to "Americanize" waves of immigrants—most of whom did not speak English. That meant teaching them English. Ethnic groups had their foreign language newspapers and neighborhoods where their language was spoken, their culture preserved. But in the schools, as in public life in general, English was used. This policy worked. It brought many together to forge a nation. This new policy is a radical change. It is bad for the child. It will do harm to the nation.

THE CHICANO SUBCULTURE AND THE ANGLO MAINSTREAM[5]

A lot of things have changed since the Second World War, but the changes have come very slowly. Mexican-American soldiers shed their blood disproportionately in the Vietnam War, for much the same reasons that they did in World War II. Some Mexican-American families have been in the South-western United States longer than the Anglos, and many have been there for two or three generations. But they are only now beginning to enter the mainstream of society.

The American public discovered the Chicanos and other citizens of Hispanic origin again in 1978. In October, *Time* did a cover story on them, and in January 1979, *Newsweek* devoted five pages to the Chicanos. News features in the press and on television abounded. Their discovery is something like the overnight success of a movie star who has been in the business for 30 years. It is not that they just arrived, it is just that someone started noticing. It was customary to say that there were 12 million Hispanics in the United States in 1978, or four times as many as reported in the 1960 Census, and that about 60 percent were "Chicano." Other than the 1.8 million Puerto Ricans, the Chicanos are the only part of the Hispanic population who are numerous enough or have been here long enough to have a clearly recognized place in American society. While Puerto Ricans are certainly His-panic and in many respects are "immigrants," they are, of course, native-born American citizens.

Chicano is a word of disputed origin that is applied to

[5] Excerpt from *The Golden Door: International Migration, Mexico, and the United States*, by Paul R. Ehrlich, Loy Bilderback, and Anne H. Ehrlich. Ballantine Books. '79. p 227–33. Copyright © 1979 by Paul R. Ehrlich. Reprinted by permission. Paul R. Ehrlich is Bing Professor of population studies and professor of biological sciences at Stanford University and the author of articles and books, including *The Population Bomb;* Loy Bilderback is a professor of history at California State University at Fresno and the author of articles on social issues; Anne H. Ehrlich is senior research associate in biological sciences at Stanford University and the author of articles on ecology and population.

Americans of Mexican descent who have retained at least some of the Spanish language and participate in a distinctive U.S. subculture. Even within the Mexican-American community, the word is controversial. While it is a source of pride and distinctive identity to many Americans of Mexican descent and heritage, it is offensive to many others because it seems a barrier to acceptance. Many Anglos find it offensive, although why is not clear. Some feel the term is fading from use, and it does seem that more and more Chicanos are simply calling themselves "Mexicans." We use the word here because it is convenient.

One of the great problems of the Chicano has been asserting his or her cultural identity. In the United States he is regarded as Mexican, and by the Mexicans he is regarded as *pocho*, a derogatory term meaning literally blemished or tainted and used to describe an Americanized Mexican. His culture is not truly Mexican and not truly Anglo. The attempt to define it has led to a self-conscious effort at literary and artistic expression. Best known are the wall paintings that enliven the East Los Angeles *barrio*, and there is a remarkably vital community of Chicano poets and writers throughout the Southwest.

Currently, the best-known Chicano literary figure is Luis Valdez, whose play *Zoot Suit* is based on the 1943 riots in Los Angeles. For many years Valdez has been the driving force in *El Teatro Campesino*, a Chicano theater group based in San Juan Bautista, California, which originally grew out of the activities of the United Farm Workers. Valdez and *El Teatro* have a long and distinctive record of bold, innovative productions performed in Spanish and unabashedly intended to raise the political and social consciousness of Chicanos. For example, Valdez brought *El Teatro* into the fields to help Cesar Chavez in the 1960s. That Valdez can now address the greater society in a play that is Chicano in theme, writing, acting, and production, and achieve financial and critical success is testimony not only to the power of his artistry but to the vitality of the Chicano emergence.

A remarkable increase in the size and affluence of the His-

panic community explains the sudden attention paid it by
Americans. As is the case with some other population statistics in this book, no one really knows how many Hispanics
there are, and the number of Chicanos is even harder to establish. Ethnic identity in the United States census is "self-
ascriptive"; that is, the individual filling out the form defines
himself. Thus a person who was Frank Torres in the phone
book in 1960 and identified himself as white on the census
form that year may have called himself Francisco Torres and
counted himself as an Hispanic in 1970. A great many young
people, children of Hispanics who used to declare themselves
part of the majority, are now openly declaring themselves as
Hispanics and Chicanos. Another reason for not knowing how
many Hispanics there are is that so many of them, especially
Chicanos and Puerto Ricans, are very poor; and all of the
poor—black, Hispanic, Anglo, or whatever—are under-
counted. The Census Bureau is making a special effort in its
1980 Census to come up with a better count of Hispanics.

. . . Although some Chicanos can trace their ancestry in
the U.S. back to the seventeenth century when most of the
Southwest was part of Mexico, Mexican immigrants started
coming in large numbers only in this century, the first wave
during and immediately after the 1910–1917 Revolution and
another starting in the 1960s. Those who stayed despite the
"repatriations" of the 1930s are now grandparents, and the
earlier arrivals from even the current wave have been here
long enough to be established.

One has always been able to hear Spanish spoken in the
southern half of California and in much of the rest of the
Southwest, but a decade ago, even five years ago, one had to
go to the "Mexican" part of town to hear it. Now it is out
where the Anglos live. When one goes into the stores, and not
only the cheap discount houses, the sign reads *"Calzados para
Caballeros"* in the same size print as it says "Shoes for men."
This is not just government-mandated bilingualism, it is simply good business. An increasing number of expensive shops
keep at least one Spanish-speaking clerk on hand. No one

knows how many Americans speak only Spanish or are more comfortable in Spanish than English, but it is a great many, and for the first time they have the money to buy the things that Anglos buy. The sight of an elderly Hispanic lady with her teenage granddaughter discussing a purchase, grandmother speaking Spanish and the youngster responding in English, is common. More and more members of *la Raza* are moving out of the *barrio*. In other words, Chicanos who strongly identify with their origins no longer feel their cultural identity threatened by having Anglo neighbors.

The reaction of the Anglo society has not always been gracious. Decades of propaganda and centuries of prejudice have conditioned Anglos to see Hispanics stereotypically, either as long-suffering peons or as brutal bandits. It is disturbing to many of them to see Chicanos selling life insurance or managing gas stations, though it would not be disturbing to see them *working* in a gas station. There is an attitude that, if they are going to hold entrepreneurial or managerial jobs, the least they could do is to speak English at home. Much of this reaction is simply "nativism."

Nowhere is American xenophobia seen more clearly than in attitudes toward foreign languages: "He don't even talk English" is the ultimate indictment of the immigrant. The gringo tourist in Mexico City who gets upset and abusive when the street vendor or the shop girl does not understand English, or the American army officer in Germany who insists that, "If you yell loud enough they will understand English," are showing a xenophobia as American as pizza or Volkswagens. By all means, the situation in Canada where one finds French, the language of Quebec, and English, the language of success, should be avoided. But it is not concern for the economic opportunities of the Chicano that outrages so many Anglos when they see ballots and voting instructions in Spanish. These angry Anglos usually say they resent the added cost in preparing the materials. They never seem to realize that the non-English speaker is taxed so the information can be made available in English. There are dangers in bilingualism, but there are also dangers in arbitrarily shutting people out of the political system.

Some of the estrangement between Chicanos and Anglos is attributable to the Chicanos, particularly to the adolescents. These young people tend to be surly, sullen, and slovenly. In other words, they are exactly like Anglo adolescents. A very few tend to form tight cliques and dress in a distinctive manner sometimes calculated to upset Anglos. They walk down the high school corridors in groups of six or eight, spread out so that others have to wend their ways through their group. They glare at people, stride arrogantly, and generally indulge in menacing hostility displays traditionally characteristic of teenage gangs. This behavior is temporary in the youth's life, at least in the vast majority of cases. It is born of adolescent uncertainty and fear of rejection by the rest of society.

No discussion of Chicano youth is complete without mention of the "chopped-and-channeled low-riders." A low-rider is a modified car, usually a big one, frequently several years old, and immaculately restored. It has a shiny, acrylic paint job with metallic flakes. It has been modified so that the body sits down over the wheels and rides as low to the ground as possible. They are customarily driven around very slowly in order to be admired. Because they are usually unwieldy, have the turning radius of a Greyhound bus, and can clog a parking lot by the simple process of driving in, they are completely impractical as a means of transport; the delight is simply in their ownership. To the middle-class, middle-aged Anglo eye, low-riders are dreadful, but what could be more American than wasting money on outlandish automobiles?

The future of the Chicano subculture is the most pressing social question in the American Southwest. Historians could be of profound service if they carefully studied the process of acculturation of other large immigrant groups, particularly the Irish, the Italians, and the Russian Jews. Given the academic historians' unerring instinct for the trivial and irrelevant, it is safe to assume that they will not. If they choose a social topic instead of another biography of Jefferson, they typically prefer to study such pressing problems as crime rates in industrializing cities in Germany in the last century. As a result there is no systematic body of information about previous immigrants to help in evaluating the Chicano subculture.

Are Chicanos more tenacious in clinging to their language and their ways than other immigrant groups have been? This is impossible to answer unless it is first established how long it took other groups to make it in American society and by what avenues they made their ways. Dwight Eisenhower, elected in 1952, was the first German-surnamed president of the United States; John Kennedy, in 1960, the first Irish one. No politician with an Italian name or any Jew has even come close. Edmund Muskie, of Polish extraction, was a contender of 1972. As the 1980 presidential election approaches, the names of the front runners are ones commonly found in the London or Dublin telephone directories—Baker, Brown, Carter, Ford, Kennedy (again), and Reagan.

Seventy years after large-scale German migration to this country began, there were scores of German-language newspapers in the United States. They were closed down by the anti-German hysteria accompanying U.S. involvement in World War I, not by the normal abandonment of the language. The process of amalgamation into the alloy formed in the American melting pot has been a slow one for all the other immigrant groups, especially those speaking languages other than English. It will be slow for the Chicanos and other Hispanics, and while the process is continuing, the Chicanos will cling to their own language and subculture.

It is not true, as often claimed, that the Chicano community lacks political organization. It is not yet effectively organized, but in terms of would-be leaders it suffers an embarrassment of riches. Throughout the Southwest, there are many Chicano political and social-action organizations. So far they have contended with one another for the leadership of their minority far more than they have contended with the greater society in their minority's behalf. Effective interaction with the rest of society is only beginning.

In the 1970 congressional campaign in one of the districts in California's San Joaquin Valley, where over 30 percent of the residents were Spanish-speaking/Spanish-surnamed, one campaign manager, an old pro, said, "The voters are over 35 and white. We will not spend a nickel on anyone else." His candidate gained over 70 percent of the votes that year. The campaign manager was not a curmudgeon or a bigot; he simply wanted his candidate to win the election. Not one word of campaign material was prepared to appeal to the Chicano voter, not one minute of airtime was purchased on a Spanish-language radio station, and it did not make the least bit of difference. Things will not be appreciably different in the 1980 elections. Thirty percent of the Valley's residents might be Chicano, but so long as low registration and voting rates reduce them to less than five percent of the electorate, the Anglo politician will ignore them and a Chicano candidate will make it only with heavy Anglo support.

At last, however, Chicano candidates for major offices are emerging. Two Chicano state assemblymen are considering running for governor of California in 1982, and a Los Angeles businessman is a Republican candidate for President in 1980.

If there were no outside problems, the Chicano community could be expected gradually to become amalgamated with the dominant culture in a sort of mutual adjustment process, just as earlier immigrant groups have done. Amalgamation is neither absorption of the minority culture nor corruption of it. The Italian community, after all, has not lost all its identity, and many of its values and qualities have had influence on the original Anglo society. Similarly, if given a chance, the Chicano culture and the Anglo society would evolve toward one another, each adjusting and accommodating to the other until the blend was complete. The resulting society would be more varied, more inclusive, and more vital.

In situations where a still culturally distinct minority exists within a larger society, however, there is always danger of social conflict. There has long been tension between the Chicano community and the rest of American society, and hysteria over large numbers of illegal Mexican migrants in the country only makes things worse. This understandably increases the ambivalence of Mexican-Americans toward illegals. The illegals compete to some extent with them for jobs, and the Chicanos worry that publicity will increase the amount of attention that Chicanos receive from the INS.

The lives of other Hispanic citizens have also been influenced by the presence of illegals. There is a steady flow of people back and forth between New York and Puerto Rico. Puerto Rico has itself become a major entry point for illegals from the Caribbean and from Latin America, however. As a result, Puerto Ricans, who are citizens of the United States and have every right to travel to New York, have frequently been detained temporarily as suspected illegals. The Commonwealth of Puerto Rico maintains a migration office in New York, and for awhile that office found it necessary to issue identification cards to Puerto Rican workers who requested them. Without the cards, the workers were being mistaken for illegals and harassed.

The grimmest specter is of another massive "repatriation" that would sweep up whomever the authorities deemed to be illegal, including "non-alien" Mexicans, Puerto Ricans, or other Hispanics. Extreme action, including disregard for civil liberties and due process of law supposedly directed against illegal aliens, might be used against bona fide American citizens and legal immigrants of Hispanic heritage. There are historical precedents for this in the treatment of both Mexican- and Japanese-Americans. Chicanos are greatly concerned that it could happen again if public hysteria rises against illegals.

HISPANIC JOURNALISM[6]

Racism, cultural differences and the language barrier have all hindered the progress of the nation's Spanish-speaking mi-

[6] Excerpts from article by Rudy Garcia, former editor of *El Diario-La Prensa*, a Spanish-language daily published in New York City. New York *Times*. p E21. S. 28, '80. © 1980 by The New York Times Company. Reprinted by permission.

nority. But there is another major factor that has severely retarded its political growth: the absence of anything resembling a national Hispanic press.

Much of the blame for its absence can be attributed to the Latinos themselves. Despite a common language and common roots, there exist fierce nationalist schisms that often lead Hispanics to work at cross-purposes. These disputes make it very difficult, although not impossible, for broad-based news publications for Latinos to be successful.

Advertising and the Hispanic Media

The advertising industry is a case in point. Because the industry was far more advanced in Fulgencio Batista's Cuba than in any other Latin-American country, it was natural for Cuban exiles with professional experience to dominate the Spanish-language advertising community here. While they successfully serve their clients, which include virtually every major national account, they wield their power to impose a form of censorship on the Hispanic-oriented print and broadcast-news media by withholding, or threatening to withhold, advertisements unless news, editorial or program content is changed. . . . Editorializing in the news columns is standard fare in these publications and those who express an opposing point of view are ignored, dismissed as naïve or as Communists.

The Cubans are not the only culprits in this regard. By threatening boycotts or worse, Puerto Ricans, Dominicans, Mexicans and other Hispanic subgroups have dictated changes in the policy or the content of the Hispanic news media. Because virtually all of the Spanish-language broadcasts and publications are only marginally profitable they have had to knuckle under. The result has been that each has been given a nationalistic identity: This newspaper is for Puerto Ricans, that magazine is for Cubans, this radio station caters to South Americans, this other to Mexicans—and none serves the interests of the total Hispanic community in the United States, either in Spanish or in English.

The Role of a National Press

The importance of this should not be overlooked. The role of a national press in developing an ethnic conscience, forming a consensus of goals and strategies, and bringing potential leaders before the public is crucial to the progress of any American minority group.

The development of black-oriented organizations such as the National Association for the Advancement of Colored People, Congress of Racial Equality and the Urban League was due, to a substantial degree, to the existence of black publications such as the Baltimore *Afro-American*, the Pittsburgh *Courier*, the *Amsterdam News* and *Ebony* magazine. These publications were not only powerful within their individual communities but also provided a national forum for blacks. There are no comparable Hispanic publications in this country.

Computerized print-media technology allows for the creation of a national Spanish-language or bilingual daily newspaper with regional editions in major Hispanic markets. The Sunday or weekend edition could double as a national Latino news magazine. In the broadcast media, the creation of an independent Latino news network is feasible. . . .

To overcome the sub-ethnic differences that now affect the Hispanic news media, it is necessary that [print and broadcast] talent be employed with a commitment to United States-style journalism: unbiased, uncompromising, hard-hitting. The exposure to a wide spectrum of information and opinion would help loosen the Cuban stranglehold on what passes today as Latino news media.

The key element is money. In order to reduce initial investment costs, cooperative printing and advertising and circulation agreements can be worked out with existing Anglo papers. Those agreements now exist between competitive morning and afternoon newspapers in many cities. The ownership as well as the operation of the Latino media must be in the hands of Hispanics. The investors must understand that they will not enjoy an immediate return on their money. Perhaps they could look upon such an investment as a tax shelter. In the long run, given the need and the size of the potential market, it will prove to be a sound financial and social investment in both the Hispanic community and in the nation.

IV. DESIGNING A POLICY FOR THE FUTURE

EDITOR'S INTRODUCTION

This final section presents recommendations for future U.S. immigration policies.

The feeling that our entire immigration system is out of control and that more rational policies are needed is expressed by the Rev. Theodore Hesburgh, president of the University of Notre Dame and head of a government immigration commission, in an interview in *U.S. News & World Report*. Next, a selection by Otis L. Graham, Jr., a professor of American history and vice president of the Federation for American Immigration Reform, argues for rigorously enforced curbs on illegal immigration, presenting the case from traditional conservative, liberal, and moral perspectives and urging a broad-based alliance within the restrictionist movement.

The reduction in the number of immigrants urged by some Federal officials is outlined by Connie Wright, of *Nation's Cities Weekly*. Selectivity in accepting immigrants is the solution advocated by a panel of citizens, as reported by Kathryn Christensen, of the *Wall Street Journal*. The outlook for Hispanics is then examined by Geoffrey Godsell, writing in *The Christian Science Monitor*.

The refugee dilemma as a world problem demanding international action is discussed by Marvin Stone, editor of *U.S. News & World Report*. The following selection is an excerpt from a long *Foreign Affairs* essay on the formulation of a humane and realistic policy, by Michael S. Teitelbaum, a former staff director of a congressional committee on population.

Concluding the section, and the compilation, is a *Wall Street Journal* editorial deploring the lack of leadership that feeds the anti-immigration backlash and making a plea for reinforcement of the nation's historic power to absorb and integrate its immigrants.

IMMIGRATION OUT OF CONTROL[1]
Reprinted from *U.S. News & World Report.*

Q. Father Hesburgh, why is a public backlash building against the recent waves of refugees from Cuba and Southeast Asia?

A. We could have absorbed all of those refugees if they were spread out, but the fact that they tend to congregate in one place accounts for much of the backlash. Something like 40 percent of the Vietnamese are in Southern California. More than 80 or 90 percent of the Cubans are in the Miami area.

Another problem is that people feel the entire immigration system is out of control. We have a law that says, for example, we're going to take about 20,000 people from Mexico this year. But everybody in the world knows that maybe a million will come in illegally.

We have another million worldwide waiting to come in under our basic immigration law. While they're waiting for years for a visa to come in legally, people are just walking over the border. That causes a certain disrespect for the law if a sovereign nation has no control over who comes, who works, who draws on social services. It's a very large problem.

Q. Will the Select Commission on Immigration and Refugee Policy, which you head, recommend major changes in handling legal immigration?

A. Yes. The policy we have is not working. Because of special refugees and exceptions built into the law, our legal ceiling of about 300,000 is being exceeded by about 2½ times this year.

There's also a great dissatisfaction about where people are coming from. There are some areas of the world that almost

---

[1] Reprint of " 'People Feel the Entire Immigration System Is out of Control,' " interview with the Rev. Theodore Hesburgh, president, University of Notre Dame, and chairman, Select Commission on Immigration and Refugee Policy. *U.S. News & World Report.* 89:63-4. O. 13, '80.

nobody comes to America from, such as Africa; others where we are engulfed by people from the same area. Some people say the criteria governing immigration and refugees are a bit racist. Many think they're too complicated. Some think they're too generous, and others think they're not generous enough.

Q. What proposals is the commission likely to recommend?

A. We may recommend a simplification of the laws that will allow three classifications of people into the country, instead of the seven classifications that exist now. One will be for the reunification of families. When I say family, I'm talking about immediate family—parents, spouses, children under 21 who are unmarried.

The second category would be people useful for the social and economic benefit of the United States. Some would be admitted because they bring special skills or talents to the United States. But this category would also include what are sometimes called "seed immigrants"—poor, hard-working people who come here the way our great-great-grandparents did, looking for a better life, willing to work hard and bringing great strength and value and cultural diversity to our country.

The third category would be refugees. This is a problem that we in America can't solve alone. We have a new refugee law with an annual quota of 50,000, but this was more than doubled by the latest wave of Cubans because the President exempted them from the ceiling. We also have three times the 50,000 limit coming in the way of Asian boat people and another 30,000 or so from the Soviet Union—also through special exemption. So it's silly to say 50,000 unless we really mean 50,000.

Sixteen Million Refugees

Q. Will you make other suggestions about refugees?

A. In the much longer-range view, we have to realize that in the world today there.are 16 million refugees—more than fled the destruction of World War II. About 2.5 million of them were created just in the past year in Afghanistan and Somalia and elsewhere due to war activity, mostly on the part of the Soviets or Cubans. There is no way on earth the United States can take care of 16 million refugees.

Most of them want to come to the United States. It's more attractive, apparently, and most other countries aren't interested in having refugees. That's not right, because there are other countries in the world that have as much land or who are economically as well off or better off than we are—Germany and Japan, for example. Yet a country like Japan takes less than two dozen. Taiwan, even though so many boat people are of Chinese origin, takes almost no refugees.

What is needed is an international conference that will devise a world solution to this world problem.

Q. How many immigrants a year will you recommend?

A. We're discussing a total of as low as a half a million and as high as a million annually. The higher figure would be 200,000 more than are entering legally this year.

We also may recommend an ongoing commission of a very high level that would look at this quota each year and adjust it according to the social and economic situation in the United States at that time. For example, looking at the unemployment of some 8.5 million people right now, the commission might say, "We can't take as many this year. Next year, if things are better, we might be able to take more."

If an emergency created enormous numbers of refugees, the commission might also cut down on the quota in our category for social-economic betterment to compensate for the larger flow of refugees. But over a five-year period, we would try to come close to the total cap of 500,000 to 1 million a year. One reason quotas need to be flexible is that demographic projections show our low birth rates will make us short of workers in certain areas by the end of the '80s, especially in the sun belt, and in certain parts of agriculture and manufacturing.

Q. What does the commission plan to do about illegal aliens?

A. It seems to me there are only two conceivable ways of stemming this flow. One is to help economic development in the countries from which they come so they aren't forced by poverty or joblessness to emigrate.

The second is to make it impossible for people who are here illegally to work. That's done throughout most of Europe. You can't go to France and get a job unless you have a card that entitles you to get a job. If you're an illegal alien, you don't get that card. It works in Europe, where almost every country has some kind of identification.

Q. *Doesn't the idea of an identity card go against the American grain?*

A. Here we get into great controversy, of course. The only way you're going to close off jobs to undocumented workers is to tell employers that there are going to be sanctions against them if they hire people who aren't qualified to work under the law.

But you can't do that unless you make it simple for them to find out if someone is qualified or not—which leads you to some kind of identification that's efficient and can't be counterfeited. People then, of course, begin screaming, "This is a national identity card." And they start talking about national police.

We can get around that because it would be possible to write into any law creating such a document various provisions that would keep it from being abused. For example, you could say you don't have to carry this document. You only have to produce it when you change your job or apply for new work. It's illegal for the police to use this document for identification.

Q. *What about the illegals who are already here?*

A. I think most people would like to see some form of amnesty for the 3 to 6 million illegals who are already in the United States: Either put them in a category of permanent residents without being citizens, or put them in the category of permanent residency with a chance of becoming citizens after a certain period of time.

Q. *Most attempts to change immigration laws have been*

shredded by warring factions in Congress and government.
Will your commission's proposals fare any better?

A. The difference now is that the country at large seems a
lot more alert to the urgency of the problem.

In this situation, you're going to get all kinds of groups
with special interests. Labor unions generally seem to be
against a temporary-worker program. There are employers
who are exploiting people and are against cutting off the flow
of cheap labor because it means no union problems and it
helps them keep up with foreign competition.

Among the ethnic groups, some people are especially interested in Jewish refugees coming out of the Soviet Union.
Others are interested in Haitians because they seem to be dis-
criminated against because they're black. Koreans and Filipinos were very vociferous at our hearings in Los Angeles and
San Francisco about extending laws more broadly so that
brothers, sisters and distant relatives could join their families
more easily.

We want to be rational; we want to be generous, in keeping with our tradition as a nation of immigrants; we want to
be nonracist. But we also want to be efficient and effective.
We don't want to have laws that are just disrespected or that
are a mockery that people simply flout.

Copyright 1980 U.S. News & World Report, Inc.

THE NEW REFORM MOVEMENT[2]

Immigration, as in the years prior to World War I, is again
of enormous demographic significance to the future of the
U.S. What is of demographic significance is of social and economic significance, and should be of political significance.

[2] Excerpts from *Illegal Immigration and the New Reform Movement,* by Otis L.
Graham, Jr., professor of American history, University of North Carolina at Chapel
Hill, and vice-chairman, Federation for American Immigration Reform. (FAIR Immi-
gration Paper II) Federation for American Immigration Reform. 2028 P St. N.W.
Washington, DC 20036. '80. p 7–24, 29–31. Copyright 1980, Otis L. Graham, Jr. Re-
printed by permission.

Without immigration, the U.S. would enter a period of population stability shortly after the year 2000, given current trends. Because of it, we can see no end to our population growth, and this of course means a different America to our children.

This volume of immigration has not escaped public attention, and the level of controversy has been rising. Not since 1950–52, perhaps not since 1921–24, have we heard as much sentiment. But there is an equal volume of argument that illegal immigration is no problem or that there are no acceptable solutions.

There are those who cringe at the necessity for such a policy debate, anticipating the mobilization of ugly passions. They recall that the restrictionist impulse of pre-World War I days and the early nineteen-twenties by and large had its source in nativist elements of the Anglo-Saxon middle class, with some support from organized labor and certain intellectuals much concerned with racial purity. Though the country has moved far beyond the racial attitudes of fifty, even twenty, years ago, there seems still to linger the assumption that restrictionist ideas must somehow derive from the reactionary side of the national character. My argument here will be that the restrictionist case can and must be articulated from centrist, and even liberal or radical, perspectives, and that it can be soundly based upon what, for want of a better word, we may term progressive social values. . . .

If we could avoid the issue, we should all wish to do so. We are all descended from immigrants, Americans because of open borders. We are not eager to be the generation to close them. When we formed our national attitudes, the world was large enough for all. For most of us, this inherited magnanimity to the voyager in search of a better life, along with a basic moral decency, prevents us from pondering the necessity of keeping people out.

But our time for avoidance of the issue runs short because of human demography. . . .

What accounts for the sluggish mobilization and the relative lack of political focus of the sentiment for restriction? It is not enough to point out that the vigorous ethnic politics of contemporary America makes the issue of illegal immigration dangerous ground for politicians, calculating as they do that Hispanic or other groups sharing ethnicity with incoming migrants will interpret concern over illegal immigration as an unfriendly stance. It is not enough to explain the muted appeal of restrictionist reform to point out that the American liberal community instinctively shuns a policy area with the ungenerous, pull-up-the-gangplank redolence which always must attach to efforts to control immigration. Nor to add that the important Jewish component in American public life has an especial emotional tie to the open door for refugees, and in a sense every immigrant is a refugee of sorts. We find restrictionist sentiment immobilized also because of a vivid historical recollection embedded in the mind of this generation.

Conservative Restrictionism

Those who mechanically extrapolate from what little they remember of our history, assume that the restrictionists' case remains as it was in those very different days half a century ago when the limiting laws of 1921 and 1924 were being formulated and debated. Restriction is thought to be an essentially rightist impulse, combining the nativist effort to keep America predominantly white Anglo-Saxon Protestant with a general inclination to harass and intimidate those minority populations who did not come over on the Mayflower. And indeed there is a history from which to make such extrapolations. Restrictionism has been a special obsession of the nativist right. This was true in the eighteen-forties, in the eighteen-eighties and 'nineties, in the nineteen-twenties, all periods of our most intense concern with the issue. These years were the peaks in a dreary, abhorrent cycle of nativist fears of newcomers. No American can or should forget the ugly sentiments which large-scale immigration repeatedly provoked in some of the "native" (northern European origin) population. (And the immigration need not be large-scale for the reactionary impulse to feed on it. The McCarran-Walter

Act of 1952 reflected hysteria at the infiltration into our nation by subversives with a variety of un-American ideas; yet
the volume of immigration at that time was relatively small.)

This history must not be allowed to mesmerize us, or to
substitute for thought. True, there are still with us those who
urge restriction out of what may appear to be motives of ethnic, racial, and class dislike, or feelings of cultural superiority.
Yet these sentiments are quite muted, for the country is far,
far from the openly racist operating assumptions of the nineteen-twenties and before. What might be called the conservative restrictionism of the nineteen-twenties dealt openly in
concerns about "mongrel" and "inferior" races, "degener-
acy," loss of racial purity and vigor, and so on. There is none
of that talk in our public discussion today, and one has to be
on the mailing list of the most extremist groups to read anything like it.

The conservative case now takes an economic form, arguing that illegal immigrants cause one-to-one job displacement
(thus accounting for almost all of the seven to eight million
unemployed), or at least significant job displacement. In this
view, every American citizen passed over for employment in
favor of a more tractable and inexpensive alien becomes a
public charge, perhaps a part of the crime statistics, so that a
bargain for some employer carries a heavy social cost. There
is also the view, untinged by any racial overtones, that illegal
immigrants impose heavy social welfare costs directly, especially in public health, education, and support for the indi-
gent. Much of these costs rest upon burdened local governments, though of course the responsibility for immigration
rests with the federal government. And in addition to these
complaints of American unemployment and social welfare
costs, those with a finely tuned ear and a willingness to circu-
late outside the sophisticated urban forums can hear that illegal immigrants (maybe all immigrants) are not good human
material. When candid, Americans usually prefer highly
skilled Japanese engineers or French brain surgeons to the
hard-working but semi-literate peasants from Guatemala, Jamaica, or Mexico.

But these charges, this conservative case for restrictionism, has not stood up well upon examination, and if restrictionism rested on these charges it would carry little weight. There is some actual job displacement, but this is difficult to measure and few credit it with more than one-quarter of the current unemployment total. In the five or six large cities where illegal immigrants have massed most heavily, there are some sizeable costs to taxpayers due to school impacts. But on the whole illegals do not use "welfare" services very extensively, or they have not been proven to, and some studies argue that they perhaps pay more in taxes (including Social Security taxes) than they cost local governments in dollars. If amnesty is enacted, then some large number of illegals will suddenly become legal. Perhaps the total will reach eight or ten million, depending upon amnesty provisions. Their families will then be eligible for entry, and the use of social services might sharply increase.

So, conservative restrictionism, prevented by the moral and political climate from making good use of any racial or ethnic arguments, claims that taxpayers are hurt and thus lays down a narrow and not overwhelming case for reform. The arguments thus far cited will not have much appeal to those who know that the evidence is too mixed to support alarmist claims. Americans cannot be expected to take a strong stance for the exclusion of most volunteering foreign workers on the grounds of taxpayer inconvenience alone.

The view that the nation's assimilative capacities are strained by large-scale immigration is another older view that makes no discernible headway today among progressive people. Fears of social division, our history is thought to teach, have always been mere rationalizations for dislike of particular racial and ethnic groups. "Social division" is code, we seem to have concluded, for racial stereotyping. It has been dogma for several decades, among at least the most educated of our people, that the nation can stand any amount of cultural fragmentation. This is cultural pluralism, the source of America's strength. If immigration reform rested solely upon the social division concern, it would sit upon a base of ignorance and would have a very truncated appeal. Costs to tax-payers and heightened ethnic animosities and divisiveness are concerns which make little appeal to the educated and enlightened who must be won over before immigration reform is possible.

Liberal Restrictionism

More substantial arguments for restriction of immigration are available. Two in particular are ethically well-grounded, have impressive empirical support, but are not well-understood in the country at large. They urgently need communication and clarification. One arises from considerations of the new population/resources/environment "problematique"; the other arises from the pursuit of racial justice and social equality in the United States. They point toward a restrictionism which neither derives from nor encourages racial or ethnic discord or ideological intolerance. Together, they give the case for strictly limited admissions a new ethical and intellectual underpinning.

The first argument is the broadening understanding that human population growth makes all of our problems more difficult, and must be curbed through some effective combination of individual and governmental action. This realization has penetrated American thinking with enormous difficulty, but it is by now widely accepted among whites of all social groups, though the idea has little visible hold in the various minority communities.

There is neither the space nor the necessity to argue this matter here. Of course, one can still get an argument about it. There are those who, having driven across the "empty spaces" of Wyoming, assume that the United States, as contrasted perhaps with Bangladesh or Japan, has not begun to approach its carrying capacity, however that be defined. They don't understand the need for the "empty space" of America to support our crowded urban population and the hungry world population which needs our grain.

The case for population limitation meets the traditional

American resource-space optimism at several points with arguments I will list without elaboration. In a global perspective, growing populations on every continent threaten and undercut economic and social advancement, deplete resources, and work an awful damage upon land and oceanic and atmospheric ecology. The United States can hardly lead others to population stabilization without joining the handful of small Western European nations which have achieved that condition—and our own population, while slowing in growth, will never stabilize, given existing demographic trends. . . .

The population issue, we know, has attracted a few of the self-centered and the confused. My point is that, increasingly and inevitably, it becomes the common ground of all the friends of human freedom and fulfillment. In the final three decades of North American slavery, a righteous and moral cause emerged—abolitionism. Abolitionists came in all shapes and forms—perhaps some held their views with tolerance and hatred, and many would not consider other social goods. Some abolitionists were not the most admirable people of their day. And some moral and enlightened people—Abraham Lincoln, for one—were not abolitionists. Yet in retrospect, abolition was a liberating, humane, progressive, and necessary idea, and tended to attract the best of a generation until, like opposition to the war in Vietnam, one vied with friends to backdate one's conversion. That, I think, is happening in the general commitment to an early balancing of human birth and death rates, to bring human numbers into balance with resources and carrying capacity.

For those with that commitment, there is an immediate step to take. Our nation, in order better to address its internal problems and to exert world leadership, needs a population policy which will join and influence its energy, economic, transportation, housing, and other policies. This would repair a critical gap in our governmental machinery and in our national thinking. If we had a population policy, we would go through our periods of floundering and ineptitude, but gradually we would firm that policy up, and move toward the interim goal of stabilization, giving ourselves time to learn how to manage this most problematic variable of which we are, understandably, so wary. . . .

Among the goals of immigration policy, stabilization would be included along with family reunification, providing a haven for refugees, labor-force needs, and others. In time, stabilization might even become paramount. Yet the necessity for restriction would not have derived from racial or ethnic dislikes, disguised as a taxpayers' revolt against heavy welfare costs. Restriction of immigration, like the other components of a population policy—e.g., universal access to family planning, information, and technology—should come in a climate of ethnic and religious pluralism and tolerance, gradualism, and recognition of the international impacts of immigration-policy reforms and the responsibility of Western societies for some part of the transformation of Third World economics.

The second influence upon emerging alignments on the immigration question which promises to make a major difference is the labor-market impact of the alien labor force. This is brilliantly clarified in a recent publication, David North's and Allen LeBel's *Manpower and Immigration Policies in the U.S.* (February 1978), a study done for the National Manpower Policy Commission. . . . North and LeBel conclude that "the most significant consequence of illegal immigration appears to be the creation of a two-class society." They argue that some significant job displacement and a general depression of wages and standards are the inevitable results of the presence of large numbers of workers without rights of citizenship who work at the bottom of the labor market and unwittingly "create and maintain substantial inequities in what is supposed to be an egalitarian society." The presence of these workers lowers wages at the bottom, prevents change in basic structure of the secondary labor market, skews income distribution in a regressive direction, and perpetuates a two-class labor force, in the authors' view. And they make the unassailable but little-noted point that such workers represent only a temporary solution, as their aspirations and those of their children will rise; and they will resent and in their turn abandon jobs formerly sought, leaving an unreformed secondary labor market to attract a fresh round of desperately poor people who will be the next underclass.

North and LeBel are convinced that Americans, white and nonwhite, would fill all such jobs themselves, coming off income-transfer programs, and out of lives of dependence and idleness, if wages and standards were raised. (The belief is hardly far-fetched. Most such jobs are already held by native workers, though there are some occupations which native labor has effectively abandoned.) Along with this must go some careful tightening of income-maintenance programs in order to mesh that push influence with the pull of higher wages. They acknowledge that some industries would automate or close, but the vast majority, they feel, would survive the new labor costs, passing them on to the rest of us in the bearable costs of higher lettuce prices, or a dollar more per motel room for the maid. As they put it, it is time to end the current subsidy to consumers of lettuce and restaurant meals, and to some employers. Taking such measures at the bottom of the labor market would finally allow the United States to complete its stalled effort to allow all of our poor, especially minorities, to take at least an initial productive place on the economic ladder. It would permit the completion of the economic phase of the civil rights movement, just as the legal phase was completed in the nineteen-fifties and nineteen-sixties.

The policy reforms North and LeBel urge include enforcement of limited admissions, combining this difficult step with recommendations for generous amnesty and for flexibility in setting annual quotas to permit officials to respond to economic trends as well as to non-manpower considerations.

Thus, the first major research effort to consider immigration from the manpower perspectives urges restriction, not simply in the interest of national economic efficiency, but as the only way to extend economic opportunity to our own disadvantaged classes. The report may be read as a call to the civil rights movement to complete its mission, a liberal logic for restriction. The costs of massive immigration are borne by workers and the poor—the short term benefits reaped by consumers and the wealthy. The logic leads to inescapable conclusions for liberals whose concern is with the American underclass.

Political Realities

. . . Since restrictionism of the pre-war era rested substantially upon racist attitudes (among other things), post-World War II radicals and liberals have had no interest in reopening the question. As usual, the rank and file must awaken the intellectuals. The leadership of organized labor has found the ranks pervaded by a rising sentiment against illegal workers, and opposition reaches even to the Mexican-American and Filipino workers in Cesar Chavez's union in the fields. The official labor movement position is now for restrictionist reform, a position taken forcefully by the Secretary of Labor.

Another rank and file also stirs—the black voter. The leadership of the NAACP and the Urban League—older, sophisticated, enlightened, tolerant—has been surprised and alarmed by the rising anti-alien sentiment from the grassroots. Like most socialists, the black leadership chiefly holds to its Debsian position of sympathy for human beings so impoverished that they are willing to uproot from home and join the American adventure. But the pressure mounts from below for a different position. Of course, there are restraints upon the growth of restrictionist sentiment in the black community. Historically it has not been much concerned with demographic issues and is not strongly influenced by conservationist ideas. There is also the mostly unexamined strategy that blacks should be in a class alliance with Latinos, however strained by neighborhood and workplace jostling. But, by all logic, the black position on illegal immigration should soon undergo a most dramatic shift. As political realities force black and Latino groups into the normal jostling, adversary positions of interest groups, black reluctance to speak will dissolve.

The Latin or "Latino" population in the U.S. is so remarkably diverse that only the obligatory rhetoric of its aspiring office-holders suggests a unified view on any social issue of the usual complexity. We might concentrate upon that segment of the Latin population which is of Mexican origin, for here some generalizations may perhaps bring clarification. Mexican-American views on illegal immigration are troubled by a considerable gap between the public expressions of leaders and community groups, and private conversations. No one knows better than citizens of Mexican origin or inheritance that there is not and cannot be a simple or monolithic position on Mexico's current northward migration. Ethnic sympathy does not always point in the same direction as individual and family self-interest. Mexican-Americans have many and conflicting interests on the immigration matter. But the interest which they have in political power through enlarged numbers has to date been so persistently asserted as to smother discussion of their interest as disproportionate occupants of the secondary labor market. Upgrading the economic and social status of Mexican-American citizens is made difficult by many things, but ranking high among them, apparently, is the supply of other workers without rights, without the same wage or social expectations as native workers. . . .

The upcoming restrictionist movement can and should be a broad alliance, incorporating moderate, liberal, and even radical individuals and groups, as well as the conservative who has no historic reluctance to espouse effective limits upon the entry of aliens into the American social stream. Solicitude for the American working class and poor is the ground of that broad alliance. Sensitive people of progressive outlook are dismayed that the American disadvantaged and the foreign poor, newly-arrived, are alleged to be in conflict. The enemy ought to be the exploiter, if we could discern that agent, rather than ragged volunteer laborers worse off even than our own unemployed! But the dilemma is inescapable, and all parties in the 1980s ought to debate it, as the troubled Socialists (and also the Democrats and Republicans) did in

1910. There is certainly today a stronger research base than the prewar restrictionists had in 1910 or 1921 for the view that massive immigration undercuts the American worker and the poor. . . . We have many good reasons to see that the main victim of illegal immigration is not the taxpayer of Howard Jarvis's concern but rather the unskilled domestic worker. Some of the friends of the latter ought to be moving from silence onto the middle ground of responsible restrictionism. . . .

As to timing, the sooner the issue is joined the better, for the passage of time merely intensifies the problems of population pressure and makes a relatively benign climate less likely. As to the manner of restriction, the influence of progressive elements in our society is required to make the restriction cordial, firmly based upon considerations of the public interest (which means a higher priority for population stabilization and for labor-market impacts), combined with historically unprecedented levels of economic development and population control assistance, and unswervingly rooted in a commitment to racial and ethnic pluralism. We must accept the idea that the size of the U.S. population must soon become stabilized; but American nationality must never be perceived as fixed in its ethnic or cultural components. . . .

Moral Restrictionism

. . . Those who, in all good faith, are unconcerned about illegal immigration tend to have fixed in mind's eye the human distress of individuals who encamp just south of the border, or who overstay visas from Iran, India, or Jamaica. Eventually, we know them, hire them, they become palpable. But a larger frame should be glimpsed. And it reaches to include much more than America's own minorities to whom the promise of equal opportunity cannot be kept without sealing the labor market off from unchecked access to Third World manpower. It includes much more, those millions who remain in impoverished societies, unable to solve individual problems by emigration. And we have every reason to believe the very reverse of John Kenneth Galbraith's ignorant argument in *The Nature of Mass Poverty* (1979), and to conclude that a brain, energy, and gumption drain works a net impoverishment upon the societies from which immigrants come. All concede that the safety-valve offered to Mexican ruling orders by the open border to the north delays a decisive confrontation with that nation's unfinished democratization. . . .

Deeper and more candid thought needs to be given to the extent to which migration in the 20th century (at least) has always acted, within and among nations, as a conservative force delaying social reconstruction. Immigration may be seen as a system of social control—if one looks for systems, not for the individual solutions which brought our progenitors here. Indeed, large-scale immigration may be seen as a sort of individually activated and unconscious triage, in which the interests of a few mobile young people are protected at the expense of those less able to move, who stay behind to make what peace they can with oppressive social systems.

It is time that such questions once again are vigorously debated, for in no other way can there be the reorientation to contemporary reality. Too much has changed since we set our minds on this issue, and then closed them in order to survive the hard Cold War decades untroubled by debate upon our most sensitive ground where ethnicity, religion, race, and our brooding immigrant forefathers are emotionally mixed.

The immigration reform movement will require a sound moral base more than a flawless program for implementation. . . . (Problems of implementation of a controlled immigration policy do not present technical and philosophical difficulties as imposing as is usually alleged, though they will require determination and wisdom, and will extract some new costs for the benefits conferred. Since restrictionism is inevitable, it is critically important that progressive political elements actively influence both the timing and the manner of it. . . . The core of a new restrictionism must be: no mass deportations, reasonable one-time amnesty, scrupulous regard for the rights of "foreign-appearing" people in the inevitable employer sanctions and/or work card arrangements, and more than lip-service to the idea of "foreign aid." As the drawbridge, in the jargon of some, is raised somewhat, there must be sent abroad unprecedented levels of economic and population stabilization assistance. Restriction must reaffirm the racial and ethnic pluralism of the U.S. We must assume that the size of the U.S. population must become stabilized, yet American nationality must never be perceived as rigidly fixed in its cultural components. Yet all of this is not enough. The new restrictionism must work toward changed life-styles in the First World, to accommodate and instruct the rising standards of life in the Third. . . .)

The moral center is the ability to see beyond the immediate self-interest of a group we glimpse only in small daily increments and in only a few sections of the nation; to recognize that their potential numbers are so awesome that the sixty-odd exporting nations could pack our nation; to understand that this serves the interest of neither world; and thus to prefer the broader good of the poor in both sending and receiving societies (and also the broader good of the non-poor), which can only come from being forced to deal now with the causes of poverty directly and immediately, to this endless temporizing with distant dysfunctions.

Restrictionism cannot aim to end immigration. But it begins with the recognition that immigration is a solution to human problems which, though it seems to have worked for our ancestors and for us at a very different demographic and ecological time, increasingly becomes only a solution for a very few. In fact, it delays the devising of solutions for the great masses whose lives will be spent not in escape but in learning—with help bordering on sacrifice from the more fortunate—how to manage where they are.

REFUGEE QUOTA CUTS URGED[3]

The number of refugees who may legally enter the United States next year should be reduced, Attorney General Benjamin Civiletti told the Senate Judiciary Committee recently.

The cuts are recommended largely because of the recent heavy influx of migrants from Cuba and Haiti, he said.

The refugee quota for fiscal year 1981, Civiletti said, will be 217,000. This is 14,700 fewer than this year.

The largest number of new refugees will continue to be 168,000 Indochinese expected to reach the United States, including the 14,000 monthly allowance pledged by President Carter in June 1979.

Other quotas include 33,000 from the Soviet Union, 4,500 from eastern Europe, 4,500 from the Near East and 3,000 from Africa (a figure double this year's level, with most expected from Ethiopia).

Latin Americans will absorb the biggest reduction. This year's recommendation is 4,000, down from 20,500 for this year, of whom 19,500 were to be Cubans.

"The reduction reflects the massive influx of Cubans to the United States in contravention of both U.S. law and our guiding principle of refugee admission—orderly processing and departure to the United States from abroad," Civiletti said.

The cost to the federal government of processing, transporting and initially resettling refugees next year will be $690 million, Civiletti noted. He praised the voluntary agencies who "contribute enormously" to the resettlement process. "The federal-private agency relationship cannot be overemphasized," he said.

Civiletti and Victor Palmieri, U.S. coordinator for refugee affairs, described efforts to halt the flow of illegal entrants.

[3] Reprint of article entitled "Cut Urged in U.S. Immigration Quotas for Next Year," by Connie Wright, staff writer. *Nation's Cities Weekly*. 3:3. S. 29, '80. © 1980, The National League of Cities. Reprinted by permission.

They were closely questioned by Sen. Edward M. Kennedy (D-Mass.), the committee chairman.

The Coast Guard has seized 1,400 boats in search and rescue operations, the attorney general said, noting that migrants could not be forced to return in most cases because the craft were not seaworthy. The Justice Department has brought indictments against 270 persons for bringing illegal entrants from Cuba and Haiti and is preparing 500 other cases for prosecution, Civiletti reported.

A report on Cuban and Haitian entrants, submitted to the committee by Palmieri's office, an interagency group housed in the State Department, noted that although the massive influx of Cubans has dropped substantially, the flow continues at a rate of about 100 per day. About 50 Haitians also arrive daily.

All new arrivals are being sent, after preliminary screening, to the four major processing centers at Eglin Air Force Base, Fla., Ft. Chaffee, Ark., Indiantown Gap, Pa., and McCoy, Wis., the report said.

An area in Miami beneath several elevated highways, known as Tent City, will be closed by Sept. 30, the report predicted, and residents will be processed at an accelerated basis by the voluntary agencies that have set up offices nearby.

The 1980 supplemental appropriations law provided $50 million for fiscal years 1980 and 1981 to reimburse state and local governments for the costs of cash and medical assistance and social services provided to Cuban and Haitian entrants. The administration report supported proposed authorizing legislation, introduced by Rep. Dante Fascell (D-Fla.) and Sen. Richard Stone (D-Fla.), as part of the foreign aid bill that is pending in conference.

WYOMING VALLEY WEST HIGH SCHOOL

OPEN DOOR OR SCREEN DOOR?[4]

Karen Smith, an assembly-line worker for a farm-machinery manufacturer here [in Kansas City, Kansas] is wrestling with conflicting emotions about the homeless refugees and other immigrants hammering on this nation's doors.

"My natural sense of compassion makes me think these people coming into our country need to have help, obviously, so let them in," the 27-year-old black woman says. "But then my sense of self-preservation takes over. The job market is straining at the seams, and right now we can't stand" any more job applicants.

Mrs. Smith, a divorced mother of three, knows firsthand about those strained seams. Work schedules and paychecks at her plant have been cut in half because there is so little business. Regardless of how needy and deserving today's immigrants may be, she feels that the U.S. economy is barely supporting its first obligation: its natives.

Around a table in a meeting room, here, 11 other Kansas City-area residents nod in agreement. They range in age from 19 to 60, in occupation from clerk to college professor. All were born in the United States. A few have had direct experience with foreign newcomers, and none must be reminded of this country's huge debt to the immigrants who built it. Each, however, is caught in a vise between altruism and self-survival.

All have been invited here through William R. Hamilton & Staff, a Washington, D.C., public-opinion firm, to discuss with *The Wall Street Journal* their feelings about immigration and its potential effects on the nation and on their own lives. The exchange is spirited, often laced with anguish, as these

[4] Reprint of article entitled "Panel of Midwesterners Advocates Selectivity in Taking Newcomers," by Kathryn ·Christensen, staff reporter. *Wall Street Journal*. p 1+. O. 14, '80. Reprinted by permission of *The Wall Street Journal*. © 1980 Dow Jones & Company, Inc. All rights reserved.

men and women grapple with sensitive issues of elitism and racism. Some struggle to find a distinction between political and economic refugees, or between educated and unskilled ones. Others try to reconcile fear of unknown, but inevitable, cultural changes with the conviction that this democracy is obligated to embrace the world's less fortunate.

Significant Caveat

On one thing, they all agree: the United States can in the long term handle most of the outsiders wanting in—under certain circumstances. The caveat is significant. Rather than an open-door policy on immigration, these panelists favor a "screen-door" approach: Entrance would be governed not only by domestic economic conditions but even by the abilities, attitudes or motives of those seeking admission.

It's a hard-line stance, undoubtedly colored somewhat by the clamor over the sudden arrival of more than 100,000 Cuban refugees in Miami, Fla., earlier this year. But around this table in Kansas City, there's also a rigid belief that the country and the immigrants it's drawing have changed radically since a million people, mostly Europeans, came to the U.S. during the last great wave of immigration in 1900-10.

Leo Novak, a 60-year-old letter carrier whose parents emigrated from Poland, considers himself a beneficiary of the nation's turn-of-the-century open-door policy. Yet Mr. Novak declares that it's time "to be more selective." Today's technological society can't absorb large numbers of laborers, he says, adding that "when I have children of my own who're seeking work and can't get it, it's difficult to understand" why so many newcomers are admitted.

His call for selectivity ripples through much of this group. Architect Ward H. Haylett Jr., acknowledges that "some of the great minds of the world collected here because of lenient immigration policies." But he complains that "undisciplined immigration of the Cuban type, where we know 100,000 people were let into an already-underemployed area," is intolera-

ble. "We can't exclude the talents of the world," Mr. Haylett
says, "but no other country allows as free and untrammeled
immigration as we do."

A Shopping Expedition

Indeed, what anger surfaces here is aimed primarily at the
government for suddenly admitting so many Cubans when
U.S. citizens were unemployed and reeling from inflation. No
one quibbles with the premise that a nation of 220 million can
easily assimilate, over time, another 100,000 people. But
many seem to want an immigration system that operates like
a shopping excursion in which the host country picks newcomers according to its own preferences and personnel gaps.

As the 20th Century wanes, these panelists frankly say,
the nation requires more professionals than ditch diggers.
Compassion is fine, they add, but it must be tempered by favoring immigrants with skills. Says Douglas Stine, a plumber
foreman: "Immediately those people would be productive;
they'd be giving to this country instead of taking." Mr. Haylett agrees, and he doesn't believe that today's newcomers
meet that standard. "We don't need 100,000 Cubans," he insists, citing reports that some of the refugees are convicted
criminals or otherwise undesirable. "For the love of mud, do
we now have to import our prisoners, too? I'd just as soon
have a few Britons, French or Belgians. I'd like to have some
Irish and some Scottish, too; we need 10 of these and 20 of
those."

Wanda Livingston, a 36-year-old pretrial services officer
at the federal court and one of three blacks on this panel, re-
gards that as totally unrealistic. Immigration, she says, has always been "a matter of (the immigrant's) need. I really don't
think the British are that eager to come here because things
aren't so bad over there."

An advocate of liberal immigration policies, Mrs. Livingston also fears that the uproar over immigration is rooted less
in economic worries than in racial prejudices. She concedes
that a lenient system may increase the cost of social services,

but she disputes the argument that immigrants immediately take jobs from U.S. citizens.

"Most of them come from situations so bad that they're quite willing to do the menial jobs Americans don't even want," she says. And as for the quality of today's immigrants, she pointedly notes: "We sometimes forget how this country was founded. Many of our ancestors were the dregs of society that (other countries) wanted to get rid of. They were criminals, too."

Divisions among these panelists fade, however, as they confess bewilderment and consternation over the inconsistencies in federal immigration policies. Linda Hampton, a clerical supervisor for an insurance company, is sad because "some deserving people" are kept out of the country while others are admitted. And Jim Collins, a psychology professor, calls it criminal that the doors were opened for Cubans while Haitians were turned away. "It's very popular again to be anti-Communist," he sighs. "Nobody cares about Haiti because it's such a small country."

Favoring the Hungry

Faced with a choice of admitting political or economic refugees, Mr. Collins tends to favor the latter. "The politically oppressed perhaps can do something in their own country to improve things," he says. "But those who are starving, there's not much they can do."

Along with compassion, some panelists feel that the nation has a special debt to certain groups. Several belong to churches that sponsored Vietnamese families. Mailman Novak has three sons who fought in Vietnam, and he has yet to resolve his feelings about that war. "But right or wrong," he declares, "these people were victims. I just feel more of an obligation to them."

Others concur. John Massman, a 45-year-old contractor who generally argues against admitting more immigrants, felt so strongly that we owe the Vietnamese a sanctuary that he sponsored two refugees, a doctor and an airline pilot. He is

bitter about the experience; both of his wards were excluded
from their professions because "they didn't fit some bureaucratic regulations" set by the American Medical Association and the Federal Aviation Administration. One is now a
maitre d', the other a baker.

"That, to me, is a waste of talent," Mr. Massman seethes.
"We're bringing people in and ignoring the capabilities they
have." He is convinced, he says, that the federal government
has no organized plan for smoothing the assimilation of
foreigners.

Typical Situation

As a destination for immigrants, this metropolitan area
differs little from other medium-sized inland cities. Of the 1.3
million residents, Immigration and Naturalization Service officials estimate that no more than 5,000 illegal aliens and
fewer than 200 Cuban refugees have settled here. "Substantial numbers" of Vietnamese and Cambodian families reside
in the area, they say, plus a "sizeable" Mexican community.

But despite the relatively small figures, 21-year-old Cindy
Lane thinks that foreign influences are changing life in Kansas
City. Miss Lane, a clerk for a local trucking company, de-
clines to specify those changes but admits that they somehow
make her uncomfortable.

"Just socializing at night around town has changed a lot in
the last couple of years because of the influx of foreigners,"
she says. "There's nothing wrong with them, but they don't
react the same as people from around here do." Unless these
immigrants "want to learn to be Americans," she declared,
"they shouldn't be here." Michael Williams, a black auto
worker, echoes her assertion: "If they want to be here, teach
them to be like us."

Even so, there is a consensus among these men and
women that the U.S. mustn't fence itself off from other peoples or impose a moratorium on immigration. "If there isn't
a golden shore to come to," architect Haylett says, "there's

nothing left. And we are, I think, the last possible land of opportunity left in the world."

Stiff Standards

But as a group, this panel agrees that today's immigrants should meet some stiff standards before the welcome mat is laid out. And the panelists are adamant about getting the recession out of the way before the borders or harbors are opened any wider. "Grown men are crying in Detroit because they can't find jobs," says 19-year-old Douglas Norton, who himself spent six months looking for work before he became a salesman. "We're trying to support too many people. We should help the ones who are here."

Above all, these Midwesterners want guarantees that the immigrants will contribute something—taxes, for starters—to the country and will immediately begin the process of becoming English-speaking citizens. John Rhoades, an unemployed auto worker, remembers working with a Mexican welder "who said flat out that he didn't want to be a United States citizen. He just wanted to work here. It gripes me that some think they can just come and work and not have to become a citizen."

All the panelists concede that these demands may be tougher than those imposed on early immigrants. But Mr. Novak, the mailman, believes he has a right to make them. "It's the obligation of the immigrants to learn the ways of the new country and to work," he says, "and it's our obligation to be patient and help them along." The nation has run out of unlimited frontiers, Mr. Massman explains, and the costs of supporting those who can't or won't work are already too high. "People coming to this country have got to be willing to put out or get out," he proclaims.

HISPANICS: THE CHALLENGE AHEAD[5]

The integration of the ever-growing Hispanic population
into the American mainstream will pose a challenge to US society far greater than the civil-rights explosion of the 1960s—
perhaps as great as any since the Civil War.

This is the conclusion after touching base with the three
main components of the Hispanic community as it is at present—at least 12 million officially, but probably closer to 20
million if every head were counted.

It is the Mexican component that will eventually force a
still quiescent federal government and national public opinion to come to grips with what is happening every day to increase the Hispanic part of the whole population. In oversim-
plified terms—and despite the flotilla of refugee boats
pouring into Miami at the moment—the Cuban component is
finite and manageable, the Puerto Rican component certainly
less so. But as for the Mexican component, it is hard to see
where it is going to end.

Mexicans are coming into the United States at an estimated rate of 1 million a year—nearly all of them illegally.
(Among Hispanics, as already noted, the phrase "illegal
aliens," particularly on Anglo lips, is distasteful. The preferred description is "undocumented aliens." Mexicans and
Chicanos ask how on earth they can be "illegal" or "alien" in
a land once theirs and still dotted thickly with Spanish place
names.) No Hispanic with whom this writer talked thought
that the Immigration and Naturalization Service could stop
the flow—despite the minimal strips of wire fence and the
helicopter patrols. In border areas the INS is hardly the most
liked of public agencies and is talked about bitterly as "La
Migra" (from "migration").

Not only is there a common border 2,000 miles long, de-

    [5] Excerpts from article by Geoffrey Godsell, staff correspondent. *The Christian Sci-
ence Monitor.* p 12-13. My. 2, '80. Reprinted by permission from *The Christian Science
Monitor.* © 1980 The Christian Science Publishing Society. All rights reserved.

fying complete control—short of something like the Berlin wall. But on the south of that border is Mexico, which has one of the highest birthrates in the world and is expected to have a population of 204 million by this time next century. The US population, according to World Bank estimates, will have leveled off at 271 million four or five decades earlier. Between now and then, these two lands are locked geographically cheek by jowl, the one (despite its newly discovered oil and gas) likely to have a chronic poverty and unemployment problem, the other still offering more economic promise and opportunity than almost any other place on earth.

Henry Cisneros, a Chicano member of the San Antonio City Council and tipped as the city's next mayor, summed it up. "Nothing," he said, "can offset the strength of the pull of the US."

His proposed solution to the growing tensions likely to result along the US Mexican border is a 25-year, joint US-Mexican strategy "to reduce the differentials to a roughly common level on both sides of the border." This would mean, he explained, a joint funding of the development of water supplies, roads, and industries on the Mexican side of the border. There is no alternative shortcut, he insisted. Asked if this might not, in Mexican eyes, smack of an intrusion of American colonialism, Mr. Cisneros said the best way to ensure against this was to let US Hispanics have a significant role in developing and carrying out the plan.

Mr. Cisneros happens to be an example of the tenuous entry of Hispanics into the political arena. Nationally, they have little clout as yet. In Washington, there are only six Hispanics in the House of Representatives (compared with 15 blacks), and there are none in the Senate. Such congressional representation as there is, is still little more than tokenism. At the moment there is no Hispanic governor of a state. There is no Hispanic on the Los Angeles City Council, and in New York no borough president is at present Hispanic. Miami has a Hispanic mayor, and two others are on the City Council, but there are none in any of the perhaps more important Dade County (Greater Miami) elective offices.

Yet it is at these local levels that the effective and lasting political breakthroughs are going to be made. As Jan Jarboe, a San Antonio journalist, said, such changes in her city are setting the pace for the whole Southwest—and perhaps further afield.

Hispanics—with the notable exception of Cubans— have not until now played much of a part in elective politics by turning out and voting. None of it seemed relevant to their daily needs and worries, particularly when the people they were often asked to vote for were not fellow Hispanics. But organizations like the United Neighborhoods Organization in Los Angeles and Communities Organized for Public Service in San Antonio have made the connection for the man and woman in the street. Neither UNO nor COPS, incidentally, endorses candidates, but both organizations oppose gerrymandering to the disadvantage of Hispanics and go to great lengths to get on the record the stands of candidates contesting elections—naturally with the emphasis on bread-and-butter issues with particular meaning for Hispanics.

In San Antonio, COPS and the Southwest Voter Registration Project (SVRP) campaigned successfully to end at-large voting in city elections and substitute for it voting by neighborhood. As a result a once all-Anglo City Council (in a city where Hispanics outnumber Anglos) now has five Hispanic and six Anglo members. Willie Velasquez, head of SVRP, told *Nuestro* magazine: "One hundred twenty counties are being targeted [in 1980] for lawsuits involving gerrymandering. With the increase in voter registration, we are going to make the greatest electoral impact this country has seen."

George Pla, deputy head of the East Los Angeles Community Union (TELACU), a Chicano organization helping establish industries and small businesses, confirmed that effective Hispanic political development would have to start from the precinct or grass-roots level and not be based on an ambitious individual's desire to build up a personal following. There is, Mr. Pla said, "a tremendous need for national leadership . . . but it has not yet emerged. It will take time." The one quasi-political figure in the Hispanic community with national recognition by Anglos is Cesar Chavez, leader of the farm workers union in California. But as many Hispanics point out, even he is hardly representative of the average Hispanic, who is a city-dweller and not a farm worker.

Marcelino Miyares, a Cuban-American businessman in Chicago, said the Hispanic community is in the 1980s "entering its takeoff stage. If the takeoff is successful the full impact will be felt in the 1990s—politically and economically."

Active politically already in national party politics is the president of TELACU, David Lizarraga. He is also chairman of Hispanic American Democrats, which held its first annual national convention in Denver in December. He said that probably 95 percent of Hispanics who vote, vote Democratic. He pointed out that nevertheless there is a National Hispanic Republican Committee, under the chairmanship of Fernando Oaxaca. He said he and Mr. Oaxaca are agreed on one thing: Hispanics must be in both parties, if the best overall interests of Hispanics are to be served.

From party politics to jobs. One of the fears of Anglos, particularly working-class Anglos, is that the rising tide of Hispanic immigration—particularly the "undocumented" arrivals from Mexico—will rob US citizens of jobs and put an unjustified burden on public funds and the taxpayer.

Hispanics challenge this. They make three main points: (1) Hispanics, whether documented or not, would not find jobs in the US if there were not a whole category of often menial occupations that today's US citizens are unwilling to take up; (2) US employers, regardless of their public utterances, often prefer Hispanic—more precisely, undocumented—labor; they collaborate, Hispanics allege, with the disliked "Migra" to recruit it or, before payday, to be rid of it; (3) undocumented workers are not usually a burden on public funds, for the simple reason that they are generally too scared to collect welfare or unemployment benefits. In fact, some Hispanics argue that these workers represent a net financial gain to the US, not least because they do not claim or collect income-tax refunds.

A sensitive issue at the moment, particularly in Texas, is

the acceptance of the children of undocumented workers in
public schools. Local authorities have ruled against it and are
enforcing their ruling.

What of Bilingual Education?

The moment one touches on schools, he runs head on into
the ever-growing controversy over bilingual education.
Anglos view it with increasing concern. The vast majority of
Hispanics want it continued and view any Anglo criticism of
it as an expression of Anglo prejudice and as an onslaught on
Hispanic culture and identity. . . . [For discussions of bilingual education, see articles in Section III, above.—Ed.]

To the question whether bilingual education and insistence on the maintenance of a separate cultural identity
might in time produce a Hispanic Quebec (meaning a demand for Hispanic separatism) in the US the response everywhere was an amused negative. "Let me know," said one
community worker, "when you find your first Hispanic wanting to make Spanish a compulsory language in any area in the
Southwest." (He knew of course that the Quebec separatists
in Canada have already made French compulsory in their
province.) And Mr. Miyares said that a "Hispanic Quebec situation" was unlikely to develop, because Hispanics are not
going to stay put in a restricted US geographical area forever.
Their gravitation toward the heartland in Chicago is evidence of that.

And yet, back in Boston—which two centuries ago fed so
much into thought to produce the unique blueprint on which
the United States was founded and has so far forged ahead—
the writer finds himself asking whether the very size of the
Hispanic influx might put at risk that original concept.

The Prospects Ahead

There are even more sweeping questions. Are we or are
we not seeing the resumption, after three centuries, of a clash
in the Americas between two originally European cultures to

shape the future of the New World? In that first clash long ago, the Anglo-Saxon won over the Latin, although the Latin had preceded the Anglo-Saxon to the Americas—the French in Canada and the Spanish in all three parts of the hemisphere. Coexistence in the Americas has not erased all the distinctions between the two, nor their latent rivalries. Each group still feels itself superior to the other, the Anglo-Saxons because of their efficiency, technological superiority, and commitment to democracy, the Latins because they have heart and sensitivity and preserve traditional religious values.

Yet, which is the tradition that attracts like a magnet? It is still the United States, admittedly born out of an Anglo-Saxon culture, but in fact representing mankind's first successful effort on earth to establish a republic on the basis of universal principles. The US is still far from Utopia, yet it nevertheless offers the best hope on the planet for developing that better and healthier and happier society mankind yearns for. That happens to be the dream of Hispanics, as their flocking into the republic indisputably proves. The record of the US over two centuries shows that it has prospered—and prospered best—when it has consciously striven to be loyal to the universal principles enshrined in its Constitution. It survived such travail as the Civil War and went forward to greater strength and glory, because of commitment to those principles.

The economic and political drawing power of the US for those previously outside the experiment (because they were beyond the border) is directly related to all that. Does not Latin America as a whole have as much mineral and natural wealth as the US? Does not neighboring Mexico in particular have the promise of recently discovered reserves of oil and gas? Yet this is what Hispanics are deserting in their hundreds of thousands for an alternative in the US.

This writer's concluding thought is that those coming to the United States in search of the dream will destroy its possibilities if, in the process, they fail to recognize the peculiar nature of the solid foundation from which both the promise and fulfillment arise. No less destructive could be failure of those who have inherited the foundation to guard it and protect it as the basis on which the union has so far met and overcome every onslaught it has had to face—both from without and, more important, from within.

THE WORLD'S REFUGEE DILEMMA[6]
Reprinted from *U.S. News & World Report.*

Waves of forlorn refugees, beyond the capacity of host nations, are nothing new. This year the story is of Cubans and Indo-Chinese and Haitians in the U.S., Cambodians in Thailand and Afghans in Pakistan. Displaced hordes around the world now total about 16 million. Some have languished in camps for a generation.

The world has grown used to the statistics of misery, but, still, remarkably little has been done to prepare in advance for inundations of refugees or to share the burdens. That is why all nations should welcome a move under way in the Organization of American States—and now in the United Nations, too—to control the flow and to cooperate in resettlement.

This is not just a charitable gesture. The U.S. itself provides a good example of how both host and guest must lose in sudden, chaotic migrations. The arrival of more than 120,000 Cubans, expelled by Fidel Castro or fleeing his dictatorship, overstrained the capabilities of southern Florida and aggravated already touchy conditions. The result: A backlash not only there, but elsewhere in the nation. . . .

America remains the shining destination for oppressed people the world over, but nowadays they soon learn that the streets are not paved with gold. Space, homes and jobs no longer are limitless here.

So it was for the benefit of refugees and all of us that Dep-

[6] Reprint of "The Refugee Dilemma," editorial by Marvin Stone, editor. *U.S. News & World Report.* 89:90. O. 13, '80.

uty Secretary of State Warren Christopher recently offered before the OAS some of the principles for a solution:

☐ Large-scale expulsion of persons should be discouraged in the name of humanity and international order.
☐ Persons displaced from their homelands should be returned to those countries "as promptly as conditions permit."
☐ International procedures must be worked out to solve the problems arising when permanent resettlement becomes necessary.
☐ Efforts must be focused on the fundamental human issues. "These issues are too serious to be made the subject of partisan or ideological polemics."

Those are principles only. The mechanisms have to be worked out in concert. "We might well begin," Christopher suggests, "by reaffirming the principles of mutual respect for immigration laws. A concrete way of doing this would be to develop cooperative machinery to prevent the misuse of vessels and aircraft in refugee migrations." [The text of Warren Christopher's statement is reprinted as the first article in this compilation.—Ed.]

The target that comes obviously to mind is a horror such as that perpetrated by Castro, who rejected successive pleas for orderly arrangements and pushed his hapless thousands aboard overloaded boats, contrary to international convention. An uncounted number of Cubans drowned, and those who reached the United States did so in violation of another international law—that refugees cannot be forced on another country. Coordinated action might go far to prevent a rerun.

Many of the goals, admittedly, would depend on voluntary cooperation for attainment. The OAS has no enforcement powers. Yet the mere existence of a mutually accepted code, detailing mutual obligations, would be expected to spur governments to mutual action.

Mutual is the key word. Development and persuasion will take place in a series of committee meetings just recently begun, work leading toward the OAS General Assembly meeting in November and perhaps beyond.

Progress will not be easy, but prospects are promising. The urge to help is strong in this hemisphere. In recent crises, Costa Rica, Honduras, Argentina, Venezuela, Ecuador, Peru and others already have rallied to give aid. It's true that some of our neighbors feel so poor and troubled that they do not see how they can join the effort. It will be up to the doers to show them that working together is to the advantage of all. And that goes for the rest of the world, too.

Copyright 1980 U.S. News & World Report, Inc.

CRITERIA FOR A NEW POLICY[7]

A humane and realistic immigration policy for the United States (or for any other country) must meet several basic requirements that are constant, and include decisions (explicit or implicit) regarding certain variable factors that fit within the constants. The constant basic requirements may be separated analytically into three overarching principles:

1) The policy must be an expression of dominant national interests and humanitarian values, representing a broad political consensus rather than the views of special interests, and recognizing that the concepts of borders and citizenship are central to national sovereignty.

2) The policy must protect the basic civil liberties and human rights both of citizens and of the immigrants and refugees legally admitted.

3) The de jure policy must be enforceable in practice in the real world; if it is not, it will be a different policy de facto.

Within these broad baseline requirements, policy determination requires a set of balanced choices, including: overall numbers to be admitted; the proportion of these who may be

[7] Excerpts from article entitled "Right Versus Right: Immigration and Refugee Policy in the United States," by Michael S. Teitelbaum, program officer, Ford Foundation, and former staff director, Select Committee on Population, United States House of Representatives. *Foreign Affairs.* 59:51-9. Fall '80. Copyright © 1980, Council on Foreign Relations, Inc. Reprinted by permission.

political refugees as opposed to normal immigrants (and how these loosely used categories can be tightly defined); the degree to which labor migrants may be temporary or permanent; the level of immigration law violation that is deemed tolerable; the composition of overall immigrant flows as to skill level, national origins, ethnic/religious/linguistic group, and kinship ties to citizens as distinct from "new seed" immigrants; and the relative weights that should be given to foreign and domestic concerns in determining immigration policy.

While it would be relatively easy to attain agreement that the above principles and choices are central, their application and the trade-offs inevitably required are another matter. Full agreement surely is impossible given the high level of special interest group advocacy in this field. What could be hoped for is a broad-based consensus that anticipates continued sniping from the fringes, and which might look something like the following:

1) With regard to basic principles, U.S. policy on immigration and refugees should sustain the long-standing American value of openness to immigrants and refugees from diverse sources, and should enhance the trends of the past 15 years away from discriminatory criteria for admission. This means that xenophobic and neo-isolationist tendencies should be rejected and the traditional values of openness and hospitality affirmed. It does *not* mean that immigration or refugee flows should be unlimited, or indeed that they should continue at the near-record levels of the legal and illegal immigration over the last few years. As we have seen, the United States is now receiving the bulk of the world's refugees and immigrants, and immigration at such levels is having substantial impacts in U.S. labor markets, is coming to dominate U.S. population change, and is stimulating large and growing opposition to immigration itself. Under such circumstances, attempts to sustain immigration levels or expand them even further may threaten the basic value of openness. Ironically, in this sense the well-intentioned advocates of "open borders" or unlimited refugee admissions may actually represent the

most serious of the various threats to a truly open and humane U.S. policy on immigration and refugees.

2) The protection of basic civil liberties in the formulation and implementation of an immigration policy will require careful and balanced attention. To date the leading proponents of civil liberties have failed to approach the subject comprehensively, but instead have reacted piecemeal to perceived abuses arising out of current or proposed laws or practices, without offering effective approaches as alternatives to those they oppose. Unless civil libertarians do provide constructive alternatives, they may unintentionally reinforce the proponents of unlimited legal and illegal immigration in encouraging a backlash against the very rights and liberties they seek to defend.

Awareness of this problem is growing among leaders of some civil liberties groups, and hence in the future we can hope for a reasoned set of proposals that preserve and protect the most basic of civil liberties, while enabling the nation to exercise its sovereign right to enforce its immigration laws effectively. Such proposals, when carefully considered, are likely to recognize that a sincere respect for civil liberties does not require, for example, that all civil and constitutional rights of U.S. citizens and legal immigrants be granted immediately to persons clearly present in violation of law. Surely illegal immigrants are entitled to all basic human rights, e.g., the right to humane treatment while in custody, the right of *habeas corpus,* and so on. Yet, realistically, if every technical aspect of legal due process, including the right of appeal right up to the Supreme Court, is to be guaranteed persons observed walking across an open border or landing in a small boat on an unpatrolled beach, enforceable immigration laws cannot exist in a practical sense. Furthermore, support for such an absolutist position implies an elemental unfairness— the full panoply of legal rights are to be granted to persons willing to violate the law, but similar rights of appeal are not given to others who respect the law and apply for legal entry, but have not yet entered the country.

A careful analysis of civil liberties concerns is also likely to lay to rest opposition to some form of effective sanctions against employers who systematically and repeatedly employ persons who are violating U.S. immigration law, since the jobs made available by these individuals and firms are apparently the primary "pull" factor encouraging illegal immigration. . . .

To protect U.S. citizens and legal resident aliens of Hispanic origin, such sanctions will require enhanced enforcement of anti-discrimination laws and regulations, and the use of a forgery-proof identification procedure to be required of all job applicants equally. There are a number of alternative identification approaches worthy of consideration; one example is a modest bolstering of the present practice that requires a job applicant to give his/her social security number, by requiring in addition simply the physical presentation of a revised social security card that is not easily counterfeited. The uses of such a document would have to be carefully circumscribed by strong legal prohibitions on its use in sectors other than employment, to prevent its evolution into a universal "identity card"—a matter of justifiable concern to those committed to limiting governmental intrusion into private aspects of American life.

The matter of amnesty for persons already in violation of U.S. law is often raised in discussions of reforming immigration law and enforcement practice. Any proposal for amnesty is bound to be controversial, since it in effect rewards with permanent residence (and eventually with citizenship) those who have violated U.S. immigration law in the past, while giving no comparable rewards to those who abided by these laws. For humane reasons, however, some form of limited amnesty must eventually be granted to persons who have lived many years of their lives illegally in the United States and have established deep personal and familial roots in this country.

It seems unwise, nonetheless, to link amnesty for illegal residents closely to present discussions of policy reform. For those presently intending to stay only temporarily, such discussions of amnesty represent a significant incentive to change their minds. . . . Finally, premature talk of amnesty acts as a powerful magnet for accelerated flows of new illegal aliens seeking to enter before enforcement is made effective, a process which will take several years at least.

Proposals for limited and carefully screened amnesty will become more sensible once the dust has settled: when effective law enforcement measures are in effect, when employer sanctions are in force, and when undocumented workers desiring to earn a nest egg and then return to their homelands have been given reasonable time to do so.

3) The principle that immigration policy must be enforceable as a practical matter requires a realistic view of the problems faced by all law enforcement, and of the particular realities favoring immigration law violation, and must be infused with basic American abhorrence of police-state tactics. The goal of immigration policy must not be to eliminate illegal immigration entirely (to "seal" the borders and ports of entry), but instead to bring the present pervasive violation of immigration laws within reasonable bounds, and to assure the bulk of prospective offenders that they are likely to fail. If the incentives to law violation are rendered low and the risks high, the rate of such violations must surely decline. At the present time, the balance is the reverse: incentives are high for both the illegal migrant and his/her employer, and the risks are low for the migrant and nil for the employer.

The realities of present and prospective enforcement efforts are disheartening. The Immigration and Naturalization Service and its associated Border Patrol have long been both the whipping boys and the laughing stocks of the executive branch. It is notorious that they are—simultaneously—underfunded, mismanaged, undermanned, inadequately supplied, riven by internal dissension, and politically manipulated, yet they are also routinely pilloried for failures to fulfill assigned missions under such impossible circumstances.

At a minimum, the standards applied to other law enforcement agencies should be applicable to the Border Patrol. The recommendations of former INS Commissioner Castillo seem eminently reasonable, one might even say elementary:

to concentrate adequate personnel, barriers and equipment along the border points and coastlines known to account for the bulk of illegal entries. There is no need for a "Berlin Wall" or a fortified border. What is needed is a law enforcement effort that would be demanded as minimal in any town or city in this or any other country.

More than a few small helicopters and Piper Cubs, a few hundred personnel, and essentially no physical barrier would seem to be in order for regulating 6,000 miles of frequently penetrated border, plus the long coastlines of Florida, Puerto Rico and other areas known to be entry points. More than a thousand investigators would seem to be needed to provide even minimal chances of apprehension of millions of illegal residents. More than an archaic non-automated record system would seem to be in order to keep track and assure the prompt and lawful departure of eight million tourists and others admitted annually for temporary visits.

Such minimal enforcement efforts would be consistent with practices in every other country, including the major source countries of illegal immigrants, and with all the basic values of our nation. Money would be required, but only relatively modest sums are involved. The entire INS budget for fiscal year 1980, including all its routine processing activities (e.g., naturalization of legal immigrants) was only $337 million. The budget of the entire U.S. Border Patrol is only about $77 million—less than that of the police department of the City of Baltimore alone ($95 million) and less than half that of Philadelphia ($221 million).

4) As to the various decisions requiring trade-offs among competing goals and values, the following appear attractive to this author:

First, it is clear that advocacy of unlimited immigration into the United States cannot be taken seriously in a world in which three billion people are very poor and their numbers increasing rapidly. At the same time, the present numbers of legal immigrants and refugees—290,000 immigrants under ceilings, unlimited immigration of immediate family, 50,000 "normal flow" of refugees, undefined numbers of "emergency" refugees—are wholly arbitrary, numbers picked out of a hat, so to speak, during the course of congressional consideration, and expanded by the accretion of various legislative amendments and judicial and administrative decisions since 1952.

In the abstract, no single number is "correct"; much depends upon the social, economic and demographic circumstances of the nation at any given time. In a period characterized by low levels of racial and ethnic tensions, high economic growth, apparent shortages of labor, and substantial natural increase of the domestic population, an increased number of immigrants and refugees can be beneficial and cause no serious dislocations or antagonisms. On the other hand, during times of high social tensions, a slack economy, high unemployment, and low or negative natural increase of the domestic population, the economic benefits of large-scale immigration are absent and the maintenance of domestic tranquillity and of support for continuing openness to immigrants and refugees requires the reduction of their numbers.

Whatever the overall number of immigrants and refugees that is set for a given period, it should encompass all forms of immigration and refugee flows. Hence if a particular refugee emergency seizes the attention and sympathy of the nation, increased admissions as a result of such circumstances would have to be balanced by decreased admissions in other categories. This would require that explicit trade-offs be made, that the notion of limits be acknowledged, that the demands of a particular set of special-interest advocates not be treated in isolation from the demands of others. . . .

In an ideal world, it might be possible to devise a flexible system that would adjust immigration numbers to changing national and international circumstances in a responsive and objective manner. Yet realistically this seems quite impossible in the political system of the United States today. The prerogatives of the Congress in immigration matters, coupled with the pressures on its time and its acknowledged responsiveness to special interest groups, necessarily restricts it to the role of setting broad policy outlines for some other entity to implement in a flexible manner. At the same time, postwar experience in the executive branch and with semi-autonomous commissions has seen the capture of key regulatory bodies by the most interested of special interest groups (albeit with some notable reversals of this trend in recent years), which in the case of immigration matters might be even more divisive than the present disarray of policy.

Hence a system of what might be termed "periodic flexibility" seems preferable. Firm numerical limits for all immigration and refugee admissions would be set, with strictly circumscribed latitude for emergency admissions beyond these limits, e.g., through a requirement of affirmative support by both houses of Congress before such admissions could be allowed. These limits could be subject to a "sunset" clause that would require periodic legislative resetting based upon economic, social, political and demographic conditions that may have changed. Given the slow-changing nature of most of these conditions, a ten-year cycle like that for congressional reapportionment might not be overly rigid, although a shorter cycle might be preferred.

Various proposals for a new, large temporary-worker program have been promoted as a means of regularizing the current flow of illegal immigrants, providing low-cost seasonal labor for employers, and offering a quid pro quo to Mexico for accepting effective enforcement of American immigration law. The pros and cons of such proposals go well beyond the scope of this article, as the plans differ greatly in size and form. At a minimum, any consideration of such proposals must be informed by the extensive European experience with guest worker programs over the past 30 years. . . . This includes recognition that such programs have optimal impacts when unemployment rates are very low; that unanticipated social and political problems can be generated and must be taken into account in assessing costs and benefits; and that temporary migration often proves to be more permanent than temporary.

5) In the long term, it will be important to ensure that no single national, ethnic, religious, racial or linguistic group

comes permanently to dominate American immigration—in short, we shall have to find fair-minded ways to assure the true diversity among immigrants to the United States that has been the intention, if not the effect, of much of the legal reform realized over the past two decades. In this sense, the large flows of refugees from Indochina in recent years have been salutary; they have enriched the cultural diversity of the United States, while maintaining its leadership as a haven for those facing political persecution.

The factors affecting immigration flows are normally visualized as a confluence of "push" factors in the sending country, "pull" factors in the receiving country, and "barriers" between them that take a legal, geographical or economic form. A comprehensive effort to regularize and control immigration to the United States must consider all three types of factors. The "push" factors are increasingly the poverty and political instability of the developing world—problems that can be confronted only through foreign policy initiatives, development assistance, and trade and economic policies affecting the developing world. The "pull" factors are said by most illegal immigrants to be primarily economic—the ready availability of relatively attractive jobs. . . . Finally, the "barrier" factors, which overall have been declining due to cheaper and easier transportation and improved communication, can only be regulated through more effective enforcement of legal provisions. Approaches to all three factors are eminently the province of policymakers.

Part of the confusion that characterizes the ongoing debate is due to the fact that immigration and refugee policy is one of those few subjects in which the liberal-conservative continuum is utterly meaningless. Some conservatives have favored unrestrained immigration to cheapen labor and reduce the power of unions, while others have opposed it on xenophobic or racist grounds. It is easy to identify liberals who have supported unlimited immigration in the spirit of humanitarian concern for the poor of the world, and others who have opposed it in the spirit of humanitarian concern for the poor of the United States. The array of political forces favoring continued large-scale illegal immigration include such unlikely bedfellows as agribusiness and industrial interests seeking cheap and compliant labor, religious leaders promoting global egalitarianism, ethnic activists seeking supporters, liberal unions recruiting new members, and idealists desiring a world without borders. Opponents of illegal immigration include many members of disadvantaged minority groups, liberal labor unions, and racist groups such as the Ku Klux Klan. Such bizarre coalitions defy all normal political logic, and help explain why so many prefer to avoid the issues entirely—no matter what position one adopts, one is agreeing with the views of highly unattractive new allies, while antagonizing old or potential allies in other important causes. Willingness to deal sensibly with immigration issues is further diminished by the ready use of unfair accusations of "prejudice" or "racism" against those urging that immigration flows be regularized and brought under more rational control.

Yet it is clear that there is an overwhelming national consensus favoring effective efforts to curtail widespread abuses of immigration law and, one would hope, a continuing (if declining) openness to controlled legal flows of immigrants and refugees. Hence the prospects for a sensible set of trade-offs are not as implausible as the loose rhetoric of advocates make them sound.

In the long term, the only humane and sustainable policy regarding immigration and refugees must be one that accurately reflects American national interest and humanitarian values, protects the civil liberties and rights of citizens and immigrants alike, and recognizes the importance of trade and foreign assistance policies for developing countries. Such a policy can continue to admit very substantial numbers of legal immigrants and refugees and to be firmly non-discriminatory and pluralistic in its orientation. And a comprehensive approach designed to bring large-scale illegal or undocumented immigration under reasonable control would go far toward promoting several desirable goals at once: assuring that immigration policy does not unfairly burden disadvantaged Americans; reestablishing the plural mix of immigrants and refugees of which most Americans are justifiably proud; and reversing the widespread belief that American immigration policy is out of control. By so doing, it would represent the single most important contribution toward a rebirth of America's historical commitment to a liberal immigration policy.

In the coming year the task will fall to the next President and Congress to formulate legislation that will embody such an immigration policy, and to find the will to enforce it. Ignoring the uncompromising extremism of the fringes, such reforms can be forged and implemented with no damage to the basic values of American life.

STRENGTHENING THE CIVIC BONDS[8]

The crisis of the moment is over. Fidel Castro has decided, after loosing 125,000 refugees on us, to stanch the flow and ease the embarrassment of the U.S. government. But before it was done the Cuban influx had pushed the simmering issue of immigration toward the forefront of American politics, and already some disturbing lessons are being drawn from the experience.

It was inevitable that the Cuban refugees would arouse resentment. They came in a rush, and many therefore ended up concentrated in distinctly visible refugee camps. They included a large number of deviants and criminals, more of Mr. Castro's jokes on us. To get here they leapfrogged U.S. law in a way that seemed to mock any idea of our national sovereignty. But more than that, they showed up just in time to become a dramatic case in point for people arguing that we just cannot handle large immigrations any longer.

The idea that we must do something major about immigration has gained real momentum, spurred by not only our

[8] Reprint of "Feeding the Backlash," editorial. *Wall Street Journal*. p 32. O. 7, '80. Reprinted by permission of *The Wall Street Journal*. Copyright © 1980 Dow Jones & Company, Inc. All rights reserved.

high general immigration levels, but also the special Indo-chinese refugee problem of recent years and the added problem of illegal entry. We now have a national commission to make recommendations on the subject, and recent polls show support for more restrictive policies.

Moreover, the respectable version of the anti-immigration argument has now taken shape. Immigration levels are very high, so the case goes, and the pattern of the immigration has given us some very serious problems of bilingualism and political fragmentation. What's more, these political dangers aren't really offset by any benefits to the economy.

For instance, so the case continues, proponents of liberal immigration policies point to the labor contribution that the immigrants can make. But in fact we don't really want the kind of low-skill, low-productivity work that the immigrants perform and perpetuate a demand for. Furthermore, we cannot dismiss the economic drain that the immigrants put on our communities through their demand for social services.

Given these political and economic problems, it would not be surprising if out in the country we developed a real anti-immigration backlash. And it behooves all of us liberal, non-xenophobic, humane types to tackle the problem and limit it somehow before the darker version of the anti-immigration case really begins gaining power.

It is very annoying to hear an argument like this, in which enlightened members of the elite attempt to contain the presumed ogreish backlash out there by anticipating it and giving in to it just a little. But some of the dangers are real. Not the economic ones, in all likelihood: The anti-immigrant advocates really haven't been able to come up with the evidence of immigrants taking more from the government than they pay in taxes, and there's not much sign either of any real job displacement.

Political and Social Dangers

But in some places the political and social dangers are already making themselves felt. You can see there how quickly

the bonds of citizenship disintegrate when inhabitants of a
city cannot understand one another, or when the cultural di-
vides grow truly vast. This country has always shown tremendous power to integrate its immigrants into a common civic
culture, but we're beginning to get a glimpse of how necessary it is that that power be maintained.

But you do not strengthen this integrative power by feeding the idea that the immigrants are some alien and parasitic
body, impossible for us to absorb; you do not, in other words,
talk in a way that legitimates the backlash some say they're so
afraid of. A better course might be to begin exercising some
visible presidential and federal leadership in behalf of the
idea that we can not only absorb but benefit from the infusion
of new inhabitants. And policymakers might begin being
more wary of federal actions that impede absorption.

For instance, the Department of Education is preparing
regulations on when local school districts must offer bilingual
education. The rules require a bilingual class whenever you
can put together 25 kids to fill one—and critics are attacking
the regulations for not being even more far-reaching. The
Equal Employment Opportunity Commission has recently
proposed rules that say it's a violation of the 1964 Civil Rights
Act to make employes speak English on the job. The regula-
tors who propose these things no doubt think all they're doing
is preventing thoughtless schools and employers from making
a foreign language speaker's tough situation even tougher.

But they do not seem to be thinking much of the fact that
policies like this only postpone integration, perpetuate the
alien appearance of immigrants in the eyes of natives, and increase the odds that hostility toward the newcomers will
grow into a pressure to squeeze the flow. For years, the country's politics and policies have promoted group fragmentation; it is no surprise that by now people are worried about
our capacity to cope with yet more diversity.

But the answer is not to give up on this diversity and the
liberal tradition that fosters it; the answer is to begin review-
ing policy to see that it does not erode the civic bonds we
need to cope with the flow.

BIBLIOGRAPHY

An asterisk (*) preceding a reference indicates that the article or part of it has been reprinted in this book.

BOOKS AND PAMPHLETS

Carnegie Corporation of New York. Annual report, 1979. The Corporation. 437 Madison Ave. New York, NY 10022. '79.
    Essay: Bilingual education and the Hispanic challenge. Alan Pifer.
*Christopher, W. M. Refugees: a global issue; statement before the Permanent Council of the Organization of American States, July 23, 1980. (Current Policy no 201) United States. Department of State. Bureau of Public Affairs. Office of Public Communication. Washington, DC 20520. '80.
Danilov, D. P. Immigrating to the U.S.A. International Self-Counsel Press. '79.
*Ehrlich, P. R. and others. The golden door: international migration, Mexico, and the United States. Ballantine. '79.
Glazer, Nathan and Moynihan, D. P. Beyond the melting pot. MIT Press. '63.
Gordon, M. M. Assimilation in American life. Oxford University Press. '64.
*Graham, O. L. Jr. Illegal immigration and the new reform movement. (FAIR Immigration Paper II) Federation for American Immigration Reform. 2028 P. St. N.W. Washington, DC 20036. '80.
Grebler, Leo and others. The Mexican-American people. Free Press. '70.
Handlin, Oscar. Boston's immigrants. Harvard University Press. '79.
Handlin, Oscar. The uprooted. Little, Brown. '51.
Lamming, George. The emigrants. Schocken Books. '80.
Levy, M. R. and Kramer, M. S. The ethnic factor. Simon and Schuster. '72.
Lewis, S. G. Slave trade today: American exploitation of illegal aliens. Beacon Press. '80.
Lopreato, Joseph. Italian Americans. Random House. '70.
Maldonado-Denis, Manuel. The emigration dialectic: Puerto Rico and the U.S.A. International Publishers. '80.
Maldonado-Denis, Manuel. Puerto Rico: a sociohistoric interpretation. Random House. '72.

Mindel, C. H. and Habenstein, R. W. eds. Ethnic families in America: patterns and variations. Elsevier. '76.

Moore, J. W. and Cuéllar, Alfredo. Mexican Americans. Prentice-Hall. '70.

Morrison, Joan and Zabusky, C. F. eds. American Mosaic. Elsevier-Dutton. '80.

Moquin, Wayne and Van Doren, Charles, eds. A documentary history of the Italian Americans. Praeger. '74.

Moynihan, D. P. Counting our blessings: reflections on the future of America. Little, Brown. '80.

North, D. S. and Houstoun, M. F. The characteristics and role of illegal aliens in the U.S. labor market. Center for Labor and Migration Studies. 1789 Columbia Rd. N.W. Washington, DC 20009. '76.

North, D. S. and Wagner, J. R. Enforcing the immigration law: a review of the options. Center for Labor and Migration Studies. 1789 Columbia Rd. N.W. Washington, DC 20009. '80.

Olson, J. S. The ethnic dimension in American history. St. Martin's Press. '79.

Piore, M. J. Birds of passage; migrant labor and industrial societies. Cambridge University Press. '79.

Samora, Julian. Los mojados: the wetback story. Notre Dame University Press. '71.

Seller, Maxine, ed. Immigrant women. Temple University Press. '80.

°Shanker, Albert. Where we stand: can U.S. force schools to be bilingual?
    Column appearing as advertisement in New York Times. p E 7. Ag. 24, '80.

Sowell, Thomas, ed. American ethnic groups. The Urban Institute. '78.

Taft, J. V. and others. Refugee resettlement in the U.S.: time for a new focus; report written for U.S. Department of Health, Education, and Welfare. Center for Labor and Migration Studies. 1789 Columbia RD. N.W. Washington, DC 20009. '79.

Tanton, John. Rethinking immigration policy. (FAIR Immigration Paper I) Federation for American Immigration Reform. 2028 P St. N.W. Washington, DC 20036. '80.

Thernstrom, Stephan, and others, eds. Harvard encyclopedia of American ethnic groups. Harvard University Press. '80.

United States, Commission on Civil Rights. The tarnished golden door: civil rights issues in immigration. The Commission. Publications and Management Division. 1121 Vermont Ave. N.W. Washington, DC 20425. '80.

United States. National Commission for Manpower Policy. Manpower and immigration policies in the United States. (Special Report no 20) The Commission. Washington, DC 20005. '78.

Wasserman, Jack. Immigration law and practice. ALI-ABA (American Law Institute-American Bar Association Committee on Continuing Professional Education). 4025 Chestnut St. Philadelphia, PA 19104. '79.

Wilson, R. A. and Hosokawa, Bill. East to America: a history of the Japanese in the United States. William Morrow. '80.

PERIODICALS

°Black Enterprise. 10:29–30. Ap. '80. The invisible invasion.

Business Week. p 86+. Ag. 25, '80. The new wave of Cubans is swamping Miami.

Center Magazine. 13:47–52. Chicanos' cultural vitality under pressure. Richard Griswold del Castillo.

Challenge (United States Department of Housing and Urban Development). 11:5–7. O. '80. Hispanics gain voice in fair housing struggle. Robert Garcia.

Christian Century. 95:1258–62. D. 27, '78. The challenge of the U.S.-Mexico border. Jorge Prieto.

°Christian Century. 97:941–3. O. 8, '80. The Haitian struggle for human rights. Paul Lehmann.

°Christian Science Monitor. p 3. Ap. 28, '80. Hispanics in the U.S.: ethnic "sleeping giant" awakens. Geoffrey Godsell.

°Christian Science Monitor. p 12–13. My. 2, '80. Hispanics: the challenge ahead. Geoffrey Godsell.

Christian Science Monitor. p 3. Jl. 11, '80. The real immigration problem: too few resources for too many people. John Yemma.

Christian Science Monitor. p 4. Jl. 30, '80. Cuban flotilla to US is back in business. R. M. Press.

Christian Science Monitor. p 12–3. Ag. 6, '80 Hongkong: powerful magnet for Asian refugees. Edward Girardet.

Christian Science Monitor. p 3. Ag. 7, '80. Bilingual-teacher shortage widens language gap in US schools. Paul Van Slambrouck.

Christian Science Monitor. p 23. O. 3, '80. Immigrants and illegals: another Wicker-shambles? R. L. Strout.

Christian Science Monitor. p 1+ O. 20, '80. English-only drive mirrors deeper Miami unrest. R. M. Press.

Christian Science Monitor. N. 18–21, 25–26, 28. '80. Refugee crisis: helping the world's homeless. Edward Girardet.
Series of seven articles.

Christianity and Crisis. 39:194–6. Ag. 20, '79. Boat people: the roots of the tragedy. Leon Howell.

Christianity Today. 24:12–14+. Ag. 8, '80. The exploding Hispanic minority: a field in our back yard. John Maust.

Christianity Today. 24:38–40. Ag. 8, '80. Palau Spanish-language crusade pulls L.A. Hispanics together for first time. John Maust.

Crisis. 87:235–8. Ag./S. '80. Haitian aliens—a people in limbo. Lois Colbert.

°Democratic Left. 8:16–19. S. '80. Undocumented workers: exploited and resented. Roger Waldinger.

Dissent. 27:341–6. Summer '80. Illegal immigration and the left. O. L. Graham, Jr.

Dissent. 27:347–51. Summer '80. Another view on migrant workers. M. J. Piore.

Dissent. 27:492–9. Fall '80. Hispanics and the sunbelt. Armando Gutiérrez.

°Foreign Affairs. 59:21–59. Fall '80. Right versus right: immigration and refugee policy in the United States. Michael S. Teitelbaum.

Freedomways. 20:91–5. Second Quarter '80. On the Cuban question. J. C. Bond.

Futurist. 14:17–19+. Ag. '80. The future of North America. Victor Ferkiss.

Futurist. 14:25–7+. Ag. '80. Hispanics in the United States: yesterday, today, and tomorrow. Roberto Anson.

Inquiry. 3:4–5. S. 1, '80. Keep out your tired, your poor.

Intercom (Population Reference Bureau). 8:5–6. My. '80. 1 percent of Cuban people emigrate to U.S. Amalia Cabib.

Journalism Quarterly. 57:330–3. Summer '80. Media use and learning of English by immigrants. D. H. Sunoo and others.

Los Angeles Times. part IV, p 5. Jl. 6, '80. The immigrant dream thrives on streets paved with paychecks. Frank Viviano.

Los Angeles Times. part V, p 1+. Jl. 13, '80. Shifting sands of U.S. immigration policy trap Salvadoran refugees. Michael Maggio.

Los Angeles Times. p 1+. S. 7, '80. Overtones of politics affect bilingual policy. William Trombley.

°National Geographic. 157:780–809. Je. '80. The Mexican Americans: a people on the move. Griffin Smith, Jr.

Nation's Cities Weekly. 3:1+. Ag. 4, '80. The refugees: can American communities help them fulfill their hopes? Connie Wright.

°Nation's Cities Weekly. 3:1+. Ag. 11, '80. The refugees: how policy developed over the years. Connie Wright.

°Nation's Cities Weekly. 3:3 S. 29, '80. Cut urged in U.S. immigration quotas for next year. Connie Wright.

Nation's Cities Weekly. 3:3. O.13, '80. An international plea to boost refugee resettlement. Connie Wright.

New York Times. p 21+. Jl. 5, '80. Cuban refugees in Jersey finding mixed reception. David Vidal.

New York Times. p B1+. Jl. 31, '80. Cuban refugees in Brooklyn learning that jobs can be elusive. P. L. Montgomery.

New York Times. p A28. Ag. 8, '80. Ending the bilingual double-talk.

New York Times. p C1+. Ag. 19, '80. U.S. proposals fuel dispute over bilingual schooling. G. I. Maeroff.

New York Times. p 1+. Ag. 24, '80. Haitians find bitter harvest as migrant workers. B. A. Franklin.

New York Times. p E22. Ag. 24, '80. Teaching both special and bilingual is required. Martin Andersen.

°New York Times. p B1+. Ag. 25, '80. Asian refugees strive for safe life in new world. Anna Quindlen.

New York Times. p 1+. Ag. 30, '80. U.S. admits problems on refugees; 14,000 Cubans remain in camps. D. E. Kneeland.

New York Times. sec 12, p 23. S. 7, '80. An institute for Latins in Manhattan. Frank Emblen.

New York Times. p A1+. S. 22, '80. Federal study finds immigrants are not a burden on taxpayers. Robert Pear.

New York Times. p 1+ S. 27, '80. Havana government unilaterally cuts off refugee boat exodus. S. R. Weisman.

°New York Times. p E21. S. 28, '80. Hispanic journalism. Rudy Garcia.

°New York Times. sec 12, p 45+. O. 12, '80. Do aliens fill a need or crowd job field? Peter Applebome.

New York Times. p A3. O. 13, '80. Mexico's count of migrants in U.S. is lower than others. Alan Riding.

New York Times. p 1+. O. 19, '80. Thousands of aliens held in virtual slavery in U.S. J. M. Crewdson.

New York Times. p 40. O. 19, '80. Economic woes strain feelings in U.S. toward refugees. S. V. Roberts.

New York Times. p A17. O. 20, '80. Slavery in Texas: illegal aliens, seafood and coyotes. J. M. Crewdson.

New York Times. sec 12, p 28. N. 16, '80. Schools where aliens feel at home. R. M. Gilinsky.

New York Times. p 1+. D. 8, '80. Federal commission supports amnesty for illegal aliens; civil and criminal penalties urged

for any employers who hire unauthorized foreigners. Robert
   Pear.
°New York Times Magazine. p 44–7+. S. 21, '80. The Latinization
   of Miami. Herbert Burkholz.
New York Times Magazine. p 136–41. N. 23, '80. The refugee ex-
   plosion. Tad Szulc.
Newsweek. 96:60. Ag. 4, '80. A costly break for illegal aliens.
OECD Observer. p 24–5. My. '80. Migrant workers in the current
   economic context.
Polity. 13:5–20. Fall '80. Ethnic group representation: the case of
   the Portuguese. E. E. Cornwell, Jr.
Science. 209:473–75. Jl. 25, '80. Making the multiuniversity more
   multiethnic. John Walsh.
Social Science Quarterly. 61:71–5. Je. '80. Costs and benefits of il-
   legal immigration: key issues for government policy. S. D.
   Gerking and J. H. Mutti.
°Time. 116:64–5. S. 8, '80. Battle over bilingualism.
Time. 116:45. O. 13, '80. The Cuban refugees move on. Ellie
   McGrath and others.
U.S. News & World Report. 89:84. S. 22, '80. Meddling in bilin-
   gual teaching. Marvin Stone.
°U.S. News & World Report. 89:60–3. O. 13, '80. Refugees: stung
   by a backlash. W. L. Chaze.
°U.S. News & World Report. 89:63–4. O. 13, '80. "People feel the
   entire immigration system is out of control"; interview with
   Theodore Hesburgh.
°U.S. News & World Report. 89:90. O. 13, '80. The refugee di-
   lemma. Marvin Stone.
Urban and Social Change Review. 12:3–37. Summer '79. Special
   issue on ethnicity and economic dependency.
Wall Street Journal. p 35. Ag. 26, '80. Without illegal aliens, industries in some states couldn't survive. Sam Allis.
Wall Street Journal. p 1+. S. 11, '80. U.S. policy on whom to admit
   draws fire as outdated and futile. R. E. Taylor.
°Wall Street Journal. p 1+. S. 25, '80. A flood of newcomers is
   turning Los Angeles into tense melting pot. Laurel Leff.
Wall Street Journal. p 1+. O. 7, '80. Mexican men illegally work-
   ing in U.S. leave a void in their homes. George Getschow.
°Wall Street Journal. p 32. O. 7, '80. Feeding the backlash; edito-
   rial.
°Wall Street Journal. p 28. O. 9, '80. English and the melting pot.
   G. F. Seib.
°Wall Street Journal. p 1+. O. 14, '80. Panel of midwesterners ad-

vocates selectivity in taking newcomers. Kathryn Christensen.

*Wall Street Journal. p 1+. O. 17, '80. For immigrants, oath of allegiance caps a long journey. P. W. Shenon.

Washington Journalism Review. p 21–5. N. '80. The special case of Spanish-language television. Jan Jarboe.

*Washington Post. p A1+. Jl. 4, '80. A magnet for millions. Margot Hornblower.

*Washington Post. p A1+. Jl. 4, '80. A myth for Soviet Jews. Dusko Doder.

Washington Post. p A1+. Jl. 5, '80. Laotian tribe starts over in bewildering new world. Margot Hornblower.

*Washington Post. p A1+. Jl. 6, '80. Cape Verdeans face identity problem in U.S. Kathy Sawyer.

*Washington Post. p A1+. Jl. 7, '80. Slow, steady climb up the ladder. Donnel Nunes.

Washington Post. p C1+. Ag. 10, '80. The refugees now: fed, rested, ready to return to war. Philip Witte.

Washington Post. p G1. S. 28, '80. Another American dilemma: Hispanics and the big border. Haynes Johnson.

Washington Post. p D1–2. O. 5, '80. The people who have fled to nothing. Juan Williams.

Washington Post. p C7. O. 26, '80. Bilingual education and the new racism. Shirley Chisholm.

World Press Review. 27:25–7. Ag. '80. Haiti's forgotten refugees. Charles David and J. U. Navarrete.

WYOMING VALLEY WEST HIGH SCHOOL

WYOMING VALLEY WEST HIGH SCHOOL